7²⁰

VENUS
AND SOTHIS

VENUS AND SOTHIS

HOW THE ANCIENT NEAR EAST WAS REDISCOVERED

Wilbur Devereux Jones

Nelson-Hall nh Chicago

LIBRARY OF CONGRESS CATALOGING IN PUBLICATION DATA

Jones, Wilbur Devereux.
Venus and Sothis.

  Bibliography: p.
  Includes index.
  1. Near East—History—To 622—Historiography.
2. Near East—Antiquities.   I. Title.
DS62.J77   939′.4   81–11130
ISBN 0–88229–691–4 (cloth) AACR2
ISBN 0–88229–780–5 (paper)

Manufactured in the United States of America

10 9 8 7 6 5 4 3 2 1

Contents

Near Eastern Chronology

THE DATES, THE NUMBER and order of rulers, as well as the spelling of their names, are still not generally agreed upon. The following chronology provides a rough guide for the political history of the area during each of the millennia.

THIRD MILLENNIUM

Egypt	Sumer Akkad	Elsewhere
Early Dynastic Period	*Heroic Period*	*ELAM:*
D.I.: *Thinis*	*Kish I D.*	*Aswan D.*
3089–2950	2900–2700 (?)	2500–2225
Menes (Narmer)	Etana	6 rulers
7 (?) rulers	9 rulers	Luhhi-ishshan
D. II:	Agga (Contemp.	(Contemp. Sargon)
2950–2700	Gilgamesh)	3 rulers
5 rulers	*Uruk I D.*	Puzur Inshushinak
Division	2800–2550 (?)	(Contemp.
9 (?) rulers	Meskiaggasher	Sharkalisharri)
Old Kingdon	En-mer-kar	*Simash D.*
D. III: *Memphis*	Lugal-banda	2050– (?)
2700–2681	Dumuzi	5 rulers
Tjoser	Gilgamesh	Kindattu (Defeats
2681–44	7 rulers	Ibi Sin)
3 rulers		

2644–20
Huny
D. IV:
2620–2596
Snofru
2596–73
Khufu
2573–65
1 ruler
2565–30
Khafre
2530–25
1 ruler
2525–2497
Menkaure
2497–80
2 rulers
(Khantkawes)
D.V:
2480–73
Userkaf
2473–2370
7 rulers
2370–40
Unis
D. VI:
2340–26
Teti I
1 ruler
2320–2277
Pepi I
1 ruler
2277–2187
Pepi II
2187–84
1 ruler
(Nit-okrety)
Intermediate Period I
D. VII:
2184
70 rulers
D. VIII:
2184–53
Nefer-ka-re
14 rulers (?)

Ur I D.
2550–2450 (?)
Mes-anna-padda
4 rulers
Contending States
2450–2378
9 kingdoms mentioned
Lagash D.
2562–20
Lugal-sa-engur
2520–2492
1 ruler
2492–62
Ur Nanshe
1 ruler
2450–30
E-anna-tum
5 rulers
2386–78
Urukagina
Empire Period
Uruk III D.
2378–54
Lugal-zagesi
Agade D.
2360–05
Sargon
2 rulers
2276–39
Naram Sin
2239–14
Sharkalisharri
2214–2190
6 rulers
Uruk IV D.
2190–59
5 rulers
Guti D.
2159–2066
Erridupizir
19 rulers
2066–67
Tirigan

ASSYRIA:
2450
Layer G. (Ashur)
(Contemp.
E-anna-tum)
Tudia D.
2360–2190(?)
(Kings in Tents)
(?)
Tudia (Contemp.
Agade D.)
16 rulers
Uspia D. (Ashur)
–1950 (?)
Apiasal
11 rulers
ASIA MINOR:
Troy:
3000–2500
Troy I
2500–2200
Troy II
2200–2050
Troy III
2050–1900
Troy IV
Eastern Anatolia:
2350–1750
Hattian City States
Invaded by Sargon and
Naram Sin
Manda Invasion (?)
CRETE:
2600–2400
Early Minoan I
2400–2100
Early Minoan II
2100–2000
Early Minoan III
*KINGDOM OF
EBLA:*
2400–2300
Risi
Ibrum (Both contemp.
Sargon)

D. IX: *Herakleopolis*
2153–2090
Achtoy I
12 rulers (?)
D.X: *Herakleopolis*
2090–52
1 ruler
Nefer-ka-re
Wah-ka-re
Mery-ka-re
Neb-ka-re
D. XI: *Thebes*
2134–31
Intef
3 rulers
2061–10
Montuhotep II
2010–1991
3 rulers

Uruk V. D.
2067–60
Utu-hegal
Ur III. D.
2060–42
Ur Nammu
2042–00
Shulgi
2000–1990
Bur Sin
1990–80
Shu Sin
1980–55
Ibi Sin

INDUS VALLEY
CULTURE:
2500–1500 (?)

SECOND MILLENNIUM

Egypt	Babylonia	Elsewhere
D. XII:	*Larsa D.*	HITTITES:
Middle Kingdom	1966–45	1850–1720
1991–62	Naplanum	Assyrian Period
Amenemhat I	1945–1771	1750–1730 (?)
1962–28*	11 rulers	Pithanas of Kussar
Senusert I	Elamite rulers	1730–00 (?)
1928–1895*	1771–59	Anittas
Amenemhat II	Warad Sin	1670– (?)
1895–79*	1759–1698	Tudhaliyas
Senusert II	Rim Sin	*Old Kingdom*
1879–42	*Isin D.*	1600–1580
Senusert III	1962–42	Labarnas I
1842–1797	Ishbi Irra	1580–50
Amenemhat III	1942–1873	Hattusilis I
1797–1790*	4 rulers	1550–30
Amenemhat IV	1873–59	Mursilis I
1790–1786	Ur Ninurta	1529–05
Sebeknofru	1859–1767	Hantilis
Then a dozen	5 rulers	1505
pretenders	1767–55	Zidantas
Intermediate Period II	Sin Magir	1504–02
D. XIII: *It-towy*	1755–33	Ammunas
1786–81	Damiq-ilishu	1502–00
Sebekhotep I	*Babylon I*	Huzzias

1781–76
Sekhemkare
1776–70
Interregnum
1770–69
Sehetep-yeb Re II
1769–40
11 rulers
1740–29
Neferhotep
1729–20
Si-Hat-Hor
1720–00 (?)
Sebekhotep IV
Sebekhotep V
Wah-yeb-Re
Mer-nefer-Re
Perhaps many others
D. XIV: *Xois*
1770
Antef
3 unknown rulers
D. XV: *Hyksos*
1720–1660 (?)
Salitis
Mer-nefer-Re
8 other rulers
D. XVI: *Hyksos*
1660–1550 (?)
Apopi I
Apopi II
Hayana
Apopi III
2 rulers
D. XVII: *Thebes*
1613–1558 (?)
Sekhemre I
Sekhemre II
Sekhemre III
Possibly 3 more
  Sekhemre's
Kamose
Empire Period
D. XVIII. *Thebes*
1558–33
Ahmose

1830–17
Sumu-abum
1816–1781
Sumu-la El
1780–67
Sabum
1766–49
Apil Sin
1748–29
Sin-muballit
1728–1686
Hammurabi
1685–48
Samsu-iluna
1647–20
Abi-eshu
1619–1583
Ammi-ditana
1582–62
Ammi-zaduga
1561–31
Samsu-ditana
Babylon II. Sea Land
(?)–1674
Iluma-ilum
2 rulers
1600–   (?)
Damiq-ilishu
7 rulers
–1465   (?)
Ea Gamil
Kassite conquest
Babylon III. Kassites
1531–15
Gandish
1515–1493
Agum I
1493–25
15 rulers (?)
1425–05
Karaindash I
1405–1395
Kurigalzu I
1395–73
Kadashman Enlil I
1373–45
Burnaburiash II

1500–1475
Telepinus
ASSYRIA:
1874–33
Erisu I
1832–1749
5 rulers
1748–16
Shamsi Adad I
1715–1676
Isme Dagan I
1675–70
Ashur Dugal: *tuppisu*
  rulers
1670
Adasi
1669–60
Belu-bani
1659–1491
12 rulers
1490–77
Puzur Ashur III
MITTANI:
1530–1495
Suttarna I
1495–55
Barattarna
1455–20
Saushsatar
1420–00
Artatama I
1400–1387
Suttarna II
1387–53
Dushratta
1353–37
Artatama II
HITTITES:
1475–30
2 rulers (?)
1430–10
Tudhaliyas II
1410–05
Arnuwandas I
1405–1390
Hattusilis II

1533-12
Amenhotep I
1512-00
Thothmes I
1500-1490
Thothmes II
1490-68
(Hatshepsut)
1490-36
Thothmes III
1436-12
Amenhotep II
1412-02
Thothmes IV
1402-1363
Amenhotep III
1363-47
Amenhotep IV
1349-47 (?)
Smenkhare
1347-38
Tutankhamun
1338-33
Ay
1333-18
(Horemheb)
D. XIX:
1318-17
Rameses I
1317-1290
Seti I
1290-24
Rameses II
1224-14
Merenptah
1214-08
Seti II
(Amenmesse)
1208- (?)
Rameses Siptah
(Twosre)
(Irsu)
Egypt in Decline
D. XX:
1184-82
Setnakhte

1345-42
Karahardas
(Nazi-bugash)
1341-16
Kurigalzu II
1316-1290
Nazimaruttash
1290-72
Kadashman Turgu
1272-57
Kadashman Enlil II
1257-48
Kudur Enlil
1248-35
Sagarakhti Suriash
1235-28
Kashtiliash II
1227-18
3 rulers
1218-1188
Adad-sum-usur
1188-59
3 rulers
1159-56
Enlil-nadin-ahhe
Babylon IV. Isin
1156-38
Murduk-kabit-abhesu
1138-24
2 rulers
1124-02
Nabu-kudurri-usur
1102-1098
Marduk-nadin-ahhe
1098-32
4 rulers
1032-24
Nabu-sum-libur
Babylon V. Chaldean
1024-1006
Shimmash-shipak
2 rulers
Babylon VI. Bazi
1006-989
E-ulmash-shaken-sum
2 rulers

1390-80
Tudhaliyas III
1380-75
Arnuwandas II
1375-35
Suppiluliumas
1335-34
Arnuwandas II
1334-06
Mursilis II
1306-1282
Muwatallis
1282-75
Urhi Teshub
1275-50
Hattusilis III
1250-20
Tudhaliyas IV
1220-1190
Arnuwandas III
1190- (?)
Suppiluliumas II
ASSYRIA:
1477-1363
11 rulers
1362-27
Ashur Uballit I
1327-1273
3 rulers
1272-43
Shalmaneser I
1242-06
Tukulti-Ninurta I
1205-1115
8 rulers
1114-1076
Tiglathpileser I
CRETE:
2000-1850
Middle Minoan I
1850-1730
Middle Minoan II
1730-1550
Middle Minoan III
1550-1050
Late Minoan

1182–51
Rameses III
1151–45
Rameses IV
1145–41
Rameses V
1141–34
Rameses VI
1134–27
Rameses VII
1127–25
Rameses VIII
1125–07
Rameses IX
1107–1098
Rameses X
1098–69
Rameses XI

* Co-regency

TROY:
1900–1800
Troy V
1800–1300
Troy VI
1184–(1250?)
Troy VIIA
ELAM:
Elamite Revival
1252–42
Untash Huban
3 rulers
1193–57
Shutruk Nahhunte
1156–52
Kutir Nahhunte
1152–37
Shilhak Inshushinak
2 rulers
End of revival

FIRST MILLENNIUM

Egypt	Babylonia	Elsewhere
D. XXI *Divided Egypt*	*Babylon VII. Elamite*	*ASSYRIA:*
1069–43	989–83	1075–912
Smendes	Mar-biti-apal-usur	11 rulers
1043–39	*Babylon VIII*	911–891
Nepherkheres	983–910 (?)	Adad-nirari II
1039–991	Nabu-mukin-apal	890–84
Psusennes I	7 rulers	1 ruler
993–84*	910–899 (?)	883–59
Amenomope	Shamash-madammik	Ashur-nasir-pal II
984–78	899–51 (?)	858–24
Osochor	Nabu-sum-ishkun I	Shalmaneser III
978–59	1 ruler	823–745
Si Amun	Marduk-zakir-sum I	Revolt: 5 rulers
959–45	851–50	744–27
Psusennes II	(Marduk-bel-usate)	Tiglathpileser III
D. XXII: *Libyan*	850–761	726–22
945–24	2 rulers	Shalmaneser V
Sheshonk I	*Babylon IX. Assyrian*	721–05
924–889**	*Era*	Sargon II
Osorkon I		

889–74
Takelot I
874–50*
Osorkon II
850–25
Takelot II
825–773
Sheshonk III
773–67
Pimay
767–30
Sheshonk V
730–15
Osorkon IV
D. XXIII. *Thebes*
818–793
Pedubast I
804–783*
Input I
783–77
Sheshonk IV
777–49
Osorkon III
754–34*
Takelot III
734–31
Rudamun
731–20 (?)
Input II
(720–15)
(Sheshonk VI)
D. XXIV: *Sais*
727–20
Tefnakhte I
720–15
Bakenranef
D. XXV: *Ethiopian*
780–60
Alara
760–47
Kashta
747–16
Piankhy
716–02
Shabako

761–29
1 ruler
Nabu-nasir
2 rulers
Ukinzer
729–699
Marduk-apal-iddina
729–27
Tiglathpileser III
727–22
Shalmaneser V
709–05
Sargon II
705–03
Interregnum
702
Marduk-zakir-sum
702–700
Bel Ibni
699–94
Ashur Nadin Sum
693–92
Nergal-ushezib
692–89
Mushezib Marduk
Babylon destroyed and
rebuilt
668–48
Shamash Sum Ukin
648–27
Kandalanu (Gov.)
Babylon X. Chaldaean
626–05
Nabu-apal-usur
605–562
Nabu-kudurri-usur
562–59
Amel Marduk
559–56
Nergal-shar-usur
556–55
Labashi Marduk
555–38
Nabonidus
538
(Bel-shar-usur)

704–681
Sennacherib
680–69
Esarhaddon
668–31
Ashurbanipal
630–27
Ashuretililani
626–12
Sin-shar-ishkun
611–09
Ashur Uballit II
HEBREW
KINGDOM:
1020–1010
Saul
1010–970
David
970–31
Solomon
KINGS OF JUDAH:
931–13
Rehoboam
913–11
Abijam
910–870
Asa
869–48*
Jehoshaphat
848–41
Jehoram
841
Ahaziah
841–35
Athaliah
835–796
Joash
796–67
Amaziah
767–40
Azariah
739–32
Jotham
731–16
Ahaz
715–687
Hezekiah

702–690
 Shebitku
690–67
 Taharqa
664–63
 Tanutamun
D. XXVI. *Saite*
664–10
 Psamatik I
610–595
 Necho
595–89
 Psamatik II
589–70
 Apries
570–26
 Amasis
526–25
 Psamatik III

686–41
 Manasseh
640
 Amon
639–08
 Josiah
608
 Jehoahaz
608–597
 Jehoiakim
597
 Jehoiachin
597–86
 Zedekiah

* Co-regency
** Had co-regency for a time

Preface

ONE WHO READS the history of the last three centuries or so scans an account similar to that which his parents or even his grandparents read. To be sure, there are differences of interpretation here and there. Past heroes may become more or less heroic; certain events may receive greater or lesser attention; the motives of individuals or nations may be seen as more idealistic or materialistic. But, while nuances of interpretation change, the basic structure usually remains the same, generation after generation. Except for the change from the Julian to the Gregorian calendar in some places, no chronological problems are involved. We usually know for certain when individuals were born, what they did, and when they died, and major events can be pinpointed to years, months, days, and even hours. Language obstacles are negligible. Almost everything of historical interest has been translated into all-conquering English.

On turning to ancient history, those who become accustomed to such precision may easily become confused, even repelled. Accounts of the same period in the history of an ancient nation may vary considerably one from another. Dates and synchronizations are changed, and even the names are spelled differently—Sesostris becomes Senusert or Senwosret —and it can be annoying and discouraging.

On the other hand, if one looks more closely into the matter, it can also be intriguing. About half of human history exists as a well-structured body of facts. The other half, that of the ancient Near East, is still in the process of becoming. Large numbers of its rulers are faceless people about whom only a fact or two may be known. The chronologies of the great states are often confusing, and their relationships to each other are sometimes determined not by factual inscriptions but by conclusions arising from examining sherds of pottery. Modern history rests on facts; in ancient history, theory reigns.

This book is designed to show how the ancient Near East was rediscovered and to describe some of the methods and theories which have gone into the reconstruction of its history. A huge number of names, dates, places, and theories are involved, and the writer is a mere professional historian who makes no claim either to omniscience or infallibility. To those workers in the field, living or dead, whose contributions have been in any way slighted, apologies are extended. The requirements of space have often reduced theories of heroic proportions to a few sentences. In such cases a reference is usually given so that the reader may consult the originals and partake of the founts of knowledge. If the work stimulates a wider interest in this fascinating field and encourages others to observe how the pieces of a truly magnificent jig-saw puzzle are being put together, its purpose will have been accomplished.

1

Nations Buried and Forgotten

THE ROMAN GENERAL, Scipio Aemilianus, in the middle of the second century B.C., soberly watched the final scene in the history of Carthage in company with the Greek historian Polybius. Polybius wrote: "At the sight of the city utterly perishing amidst the flames, Scipio burst into tears, and stood long reflecting on the inevitable change which awaits cities, nations and dynasties. . . . This, he thought, had befallen Ilium, and the once mighty empires of the Assyrians, Medes, Persians, and that of Macedonia lately so splendid. He grasped me by the hand and said: 'O Polybius, it is a grand thing, but I feel terror and dread, lest someone should one day give the same order about my own native city.' "

The makers of history are usually so busy and involved in contemporary concerns that they rarely find time to reflect philosophically on the past. Indeed, the whole passage sounds more like Polybius than Scipio, for the former was a Greek, and the Greeks, perhaps more than any other people, were impressed with the cyclical nature of human affairs and the inevitability of the rise and fall of nations.

Be this as it may, the scene described took place more than

two millennia ago, yet in his inventory of fallen empires Scipio made no mention of the Sumerians, Akkadians, Babylonians, Egyptians, Hittites, and Mitannians, all of whom, as well as some others, had held the center of the imperial stage for varying periods of time before retiring into historical obscurity. The fires had long since died down over the ashes of their capitals, the elements had dissolved their mud-brick structures, and the winds had come and blown dust over the smoldering ashes, layer by layer, until what once had been centers of vital political and economic importance were soundless mounds over which people walked quite unaware of the origins of the formations.

The doers in history do not wish to be forgotten, and the illustrious beings who had created the ancient cities and empires longed to find their niches in the collective memory of mankind. During the days of their glory, they drew up annals recording their conquests, bragged of their accomplishments on clay tablets and steles, built palaces to display their magnificence, cut their features into the hardest stone, and, especially in Egypt, went to great lengths to preserve their physical remains. It was all in vain. Among the ancient potentates, the only ones who were wholly successful in forcing later generations to remember them were the pyramid builders; their monuments always attracted attention and were vast enough to survive even the insensitive road-builders and lime-gatherers of later generations.

That the accomplishments of these peoples who occupied more than half of all recorded human history entitle them to an honored place in the memory of mankind no one would seriously dispute. Under their leadership, the cultural bases of civilized life had been laid, essential business and commercial practices had been discovered, most of the metallurgical techniques prior to the age of steel had been acquired, complex and even sophisticated societies had flourished, state structures of many types had been created, wars had been fought and military technology developed, and peace treaties and nonaggression pacts had been signed. Almost all of these developments were the work of people who spoke one or another of the Semitic dialects, or, even earlier, of peoples speaking languages whose affinites even today have not been satisfactorily established.

If a people is to be remembered, they must record their activities in a language that can be understood in writing that can be deciphered; and, in the linguistic sense, the ancient world ended in the sixth century B.C. when the Indo-European Persians took over the entire area. Next, the Macedonians came in the fourth century B.C. and had turned the Near East into an extension of the Greek culture. Finally, the Roman legions invaded the area in the first century B.C., and brought their Latin language with them. Languages change over the centuries, and the older languages of the Middle East would have undergone an evolution even if successive waves of Indo-Europeans had not mastered their homelands. As it was, the early forms of writing fell into disuse, other dialects became the common speech, and many of the older languages died a natural death.

Historical Recollections of the Greco-Roman Period

Here and there, however, some stray and tantalizing facts regarding the ancient people managed to survive the linguistic holocaust. Perhaps the major source of such information during the early centuries of the Christian era was the Old Testament of the Hebrew people. The oldest version of its sacred books was the Septuagint Bible, written in Alexandrian Greek in the third century B.C. and named for the tradition that it was the work of seventy-two Jewish translators accomplished in seventy-two days. Modern biblical critics cast doubts on this tradition, but concede that it was probably the work of Alexandrian Jews undertaken at the behest of the Hellenistic ruler of Egypt, Ptolemy Philadelphus. Other translations subsequently appeared, but this one had the widest acceptance for a considerable period.

While the Old Testament was not meant to be an historical document in the usual sense of that term, during their lengthy history the Hebrews had come into contact with many of the important peoples of the second and first millennia B.C. Abraham associated with a large number of groups throughout the Fertile Crescent whose names were faithfully recorded in Genesis. From Joseph to Moses, the Egyptians were involved, then came the Canaanites and Philistines, and, during the period of the Hebrew Kingdom, Syria, Egypt, and even Arabia figured in the story. During the centuries after the schism of the Hebrew Kingdom, Israel and Judah had political relationships, as often as not violent, with the Egyptians, Assyrians, Chaldaeans, and Persians. The Old Testament contained the names of some prominent rulers of those nations whose historical identities were thus preserved as figures in Jewish history.

In the first century B.C. a Romanized Jew named Flavius Josephus wrote a work called the *Antiquities of the Jews,* which attempted to cover their entire history from the time of creation down to his own century. While his work has been of value to those interested in the centuries just preceding the Christian era, it threw little light on the earlier events of Jewish history which have been so controversial and difficult to fit into the general chronology.

The Greeks first clashed with the rulers of the Middle East in the fifth century B.C., and these Persian Wars inspired the "Father of History," as Herodotus has been called, to take a first-hand look at the peoples who formed part of the empire that the Greeks had recently defeated. Thus, Herodotus' interest in the ancient peoples, like that of Josephus, was incidental to a larger purpose—in this case, to discover why the Persians and Greeks had gone to war.

Later historians do not apologize for having such a father.

True, Herodotus was interested in trivia and recorded many tall tales, but in his writings he usually attempted to distinguish between fact and fiction. Insofar as ancient history is concerned, Book II of his nine volumes is the most interesting because it deals with Egypt and was based on the historical recollections of the Egyptians, usually priests, whom he interviewed in his travels. They "deemed themselves to be the oldest nation on earth," he noted in one place; in another, "The priests told me that Min was the first king of Egypt, and that first he separated Memphis from the Nile by a dam. . . . After him came three hundred and thirty kings, whose names the priests recited from a papyrus roll." Herodotus unfortunately did not make a record of the list, but the few rulers preserved by him included Cheops, Chephren, and Mycerinus, names still used today by some writers for the builders of the Great Pyramids. No connected history of Egypt emerged from the writings of Herodotus, and perhaps the greatest value of his work lies in recording the fifth century Egyptian memory of their glorious past, a memory so garbled and mixed with fable as to be almost valueless.

About two centuries after Herodotus, Egypt had been conquered by the Macedonians, who were saturated with Greek culture and considered themselves to be the leaders of the Greek world. The Macedonian ruler of Egypt, Ptolemy II, an ancestor of the better-known Cleopatra, shared the Greek interest in the past and asked a learned Egyptian priest to compile a history of his nation.

The priest's name was Manetho, and he undertook his task with considerable energy and ability. Possibly using the same papyrus that the priests had shown to Herodotus, Manetho compiled an outline history of his nation which consisted of thirty dynasties, and provided enough names of rulers to carry the narrative far back into the childhood of mankind. His general outline is still in use today. Unfortunately, however, the history that he wrote was lost, and his work is known mostly from the paraphrases found in the writings of a third century Christian historian named Sextus Julius Africanus, and those of Eusebius of Caesarea, the "Father of Church History."

This same Greek spirit of inquiry was displayed also by the descendant of another Macedonian general, Antiochus I, who ruled Syria during part of the third century B.C. To construct a history of Babylonia, he chose a priest named Berosus. It was a task far more difficult than that which faced Manetho, for the Tigris-Euphrates Valley constantly attracted new and warlike peoples. Berosus nevertheless faced up to it and produced a history that went back to the time of creation; but his work, like that of Manetho, was lost. In this case, it is known in part through the writings of Josephus, Eusebius, and George of Synkellos. Berosus' command of Greek was poor, and modern historians have looked askance at the names he provided (though some, such as Sidney Smith, found Berosus to be quite helpful).

To list all of the writers of this period who made references to the early peoples would be tedious and not very illuminating. The Greek Ktesias and the Sicilian Diodorus are usually mentioned in surveys such as this, but neither made serious contributions to our knowledge of the ancient world.

The Greek intellectual curiosity of the Hellenistic period tended to slack off once the Romans came to dominate the Levant. Lingering on as a survivor of the earlier period, however, was Ptolemy, a native Egyptian of Greek ancestry who made a lasting reputation as a scientist, astronomer, and geographer in the second century A.D. His unique contribution to ancient history is called the "Ptolemaic Canon," and it deserves something beyond mere mention.

Astrology had played its role in the Babylonian culture as far back at least as 2000 B.C. The Babylonians drew their hypothetical belt across the skies to include the orbits of the sun, the moon, and the then-known planets, as well as groups of stars, and divided it into twelve segments named for the constellations. The map that they drew, however, did not remain fixed. Because of what is called the precession of the equinoxes, the signs of the zodiac move westward, and after some two thousand years, they moved a full segment. When the zodiac was first drawn up, the vernal equinox (March) took place when the sun was in the direction of Taurus, but by 747 B.C. it was in the direction of Aries. This change marked an epoch in the ancient world.

Ptolemy took note of this change, said to have occurred during the first year of the reign of the Babylonian ruler Nabu-nasir. He had on hand the reign lengths of subsequent rulers, whom he divided into four groups—the Assyrian-Mede, the Persian, the Greek, and the Roman—and added up their reigns back to Nabu-nasir. He calculated the date this event took place according to the Roman calendar, and it was subsequently translated into the Christian calendar as 747 B.C. His chronology, the Ptolemaic Canon, has proved useful to the chronologists of modern times. Richard A. Parker, for example, made use of it in drawing up his definitive Babylonian chronology in 1950.

We cannot leave this subject without noting that Robert P. Newton of Johns Hopkins recently (1977) published "The Crime of Claudius Ptolemy" in which this ancient authority is called a fraud. Defenders of Ptolemy reply that he was guilty mainly of publishing selective data that would support his theories, a tactic not unknown among modern scientists.

As we list the studies of the ancient peoples made by the Greco-Roman scholars one might conclude that they were by no means forgotten and that a considerable body of information concerning them was available to curious intellectuals. This is partly true. A body of facts (well leavened with fables) had been rediscovered, but the process of forgetting was already well along. Furthermore, in those days before printing presses and xerox machines, the manuscripts were available to scholars only in limited quantities, and, of course, there had to be scholars who would be interested in reading them.

The Reorientation of Historical Thought

The crushing blow that virtually blotted out all memory of the ancient empires of the Middle East fell in the seventh century A.D. when the entire area, save for Persia, was overrun by the Arabs, who implanted deeply their vigorous and warlike Moslem faith. Not that the Arabs were barbarians. They were far from that. For three centuries or so after their conquests, a brilliant civilization came into being, complete with notable intellectuals and even scientists, but it was a Moslem civilization that regarded the idolatry of the early peoples with horror. Their new era had begun with Mohammed's flight from Mecca to Medina, and they regarded the period of his life and that of his immediate successors as the golden age of history. The successors of the Arabs in the Moslem world were the Ottoman Turks, a people sometimes described as brilliant in adversity and utterly sterile in their triumphs.

Under the new leadership in the Middle East, the past was deemed unimportant and was ignored. The gardens of the Tigris-Euphrates Valley disappeared, and this former blessed land became a waste of swamps and sand, a plain dotted with melancholy mounds where Bedouin tribes carried on their wars with one another. Traditions still clung to some of these mounds, and the Arab place designations sometimes suggested the names of ancient cities. But to the people of the area, the mounds were regarded as sources of bricks, stone, or other materials that might be used to fill contemporary needs. In Egypt, where tomb robbing had always been an occupation, almost all of the graves of wealthy people were violated, and some limestone temples were literally appropriated block by block. An early treasure seeker named Belzoni was shocked at the indifference of contemporary Egyptians toward ancient art. He told of opening a beautifully decorated tomb when an Egyptian official, hoping to share in recovered treasure, quickly appeared on the scene and was deeply disappointed when none proved to be available. With Italian enthusiasm Belzoni drew his attention to the magnificent art, to which the official replied: "This would be a good place for a harem as the women would have something to look at."

In Europe after the Western Roman Empire had been overthrown and supplanted by the German tribal states in the fifth century A.D., purely secular scholarship died away. As St. Ambrose put it on one occasion: "To discuss the nature and position of the earth does not help us in our hope of life to come." To pursue learning as an end in itself was regarded as a waste of time, and the pious scholars of the period directed their energies to studying the scriptures in search of hidden and allegorical meanings in its passages. Their historical outlook was determined by Daniel 2:37-40, which briefly reviewed the empires of the past ending with that of Rome, thought then to be the final political state possible.

Why Near Eastern Interest Revived in Europe

It was from a dispute within the Church that an interest in the past was again awakened in Europe. In the early sixteenth century, a German scholar named Johannes Reuchlin boldly advocated the study of the manuscripts of Jewish theologians believed to have been written early in the Christian era as a means of further illuminating the Christian tradition. For this advocacy Reuchlin was attacked in his own time, but today he is honored as a founder of Near Eastern studies. About the same time, Martin Luther sought to buttress his doctrines by a literal interpretation of the Bible and called attention to the history of the Christian Church itself. During the century and a half of bitter controversy that followed, the Holy Writ was examined and reexamined by ever larger numbers of individual interpreters.

The religious controversies degenerated into a series of dreary religious wars which occupied European attention until the mid-seventeenth century, after which, partly in reaction to the endless religious disputes, the first age of science opened up. Great strides were made in the physical sciences; new worlds were discovered by the microscope and the improved telescope. It was an Age of Reason which was unwilling to accept much on faith, and this meant that the religionists were put on the defensive while some of the deistic rationalist philosophers attacked the Bible, and particularly the Old Testament, with gusto.

Other forces were mounting to direct European attention to the Middle East. The decline of the Ottoman Empire and its traditional hostility to Europeans permitted travellers to go to the Holy Land, Egypt, and the Tigris-Euphrates Valley in unprecedented numbers, providing they would brave the lawlessness that existed in many parts of those areas. Many did so, and reported back to Europe in highly saleable accounts of their adventures. During the second half of the eighteenth century, the British East India Company achieved stunning successes in India and displayed a lively and continuing interest in the territories which lay between that subcontinent and England.

By and large, the religious and intellectual interests were predominant. Were the personalities, peoples, and events of the Old Testament merely fables, inventions of Jewish priests some time in the past, or did they have a firm historical basis? This could be argued back and forth in literary circles ad nauseam without either side convincing the other. The final answer, if one could be found, lay not in the salons of Paris, London, Rome, or Berlin, but in the mounds of the Middle East. What evidence did they hide? What hard facts might they reveal? True, there was a strong interest in the history of all the buried peoples, but at the bottom was the lingering hope that the history of the Jews might be reconstructed and the accuracy of the Holy Writ on which the ethics and outlook of the West were based might be decided once and for all.

2

The Treasure Hunters

THE HUNDRED YEARS after the fall of Napoleon in 1815 found Europe in its most expansive mood, expansive in every area —politically, geographically, industrially, intellectually, and religiously. It was a time of daring and adventure, of willingness to accept the sobering casualties arising from the exploration of West Africa and the Arctic, of striving to make new and brilliant history and resurrecting that of the past. It was also a period of private enterprise. The same spirit that built the railways and steel mills brought to life the mounds of the Middle East.

In 1798 Napoleon dreamed of attacking British power in India from bases in the Middle East and landed an army in Egypt. His project was impracticable and did not prosper, but the consequences of his occupation insofar as ancient history was concerned were far-reaching. Among those who accompanied Napoleon on this expedition was an artist, diplomat, and pilferer of artifacts for the Louvre Museum named Dominique Vivant Denon. During 1809–1813 he published a huge, multi-volumed, charmingly illustrated study of Egypt which had a powerful impact on European consciousness of that nation.

While working on fortifications at Rosetta near Alexandria, a French artillery officer came upon a black granite slab subsequently to be known as the Rosetta Stone and to play a major role in the decipherment of Egyptian hieroglyphs. Much more obscure was the discovery of the Turin Papyrus, the most comprehensive of the Egyptian king lists. The papyrus found its way into the possession of the king of Sardinia, who had no idea of its value and shipped it to Turin without proper packing. It fell into fragments, and its attempted restoration in 1826 was badly carried out. Even more obscure are the origins of the Palermo Stone which listed the rulers both of the predynastic age of Egypt and others down to the middle of Dynasty V. A fragment of it showed up in the Palermo Museum in 1877, while other pieces found their way to Cairo and London. Had the value of the Turin Papyrus and the Palermo Stone been realized at the time of their discovery, our knowledge of Egyptian chronology would have rested on sounder foundations.

To understand the antiquarian activities in Egypt, especially during the earlier part of the nineteenth century, one must begin with the profit motive. Antiquities were a business in which both Egyptians and Europeans participated with eagerness and imagination. The country was governed by a Macedonian, named Mehemet Ali, who cared nothing about Egypt's past. Governmental officials were primarily interested in sharing in finds of precious metals or saleable items. This attitude was nothing new in Egypt, where tombs had always been sources of plunder. Indeed, almost all of the graves of the ancient Egyptians had long since been violated, often with the connivance of their priestly keepers while the memory of the burials was still fresh, and much of what the native Egyptians missed, their Arab conquerors had discovered. So, when the European excavator Emil Burgsch noted that he had three hundred Arabs working for him and every one a thief, the situation was by no means unprecedented. Both the general population of Egypt and those who worked for the Europeans realized they could dispose of ancient artifacts to antiquities dealers at Cairo or elsewhere, and, unless they were paid the going market price by the excavators, they would conceal their finds and dispose of them on the open market.

Such a materialistic attitude was by no means missing among the European excavators of the nineteenth century, whose primary motive was to come up with striking "exportable artifacts" to decorate the museums of their respective nations. At times the competition was fierce. "Those were the great days of excavating," Howard Carter once observed. "Anything to which a fancy was taken . . . was simply appropriated, and if there was a difference with a brother excavator, one laid for him with a gun." If we imagine the nineteenth century archaeological expeditions as sedate and scholarly, devoted to resurrecting the history of the past, we would be wide of the mark. The excavators exhibited the same energy, purposefulness, and often ruthlessness that characterized some of the contemporary captains of European and American industry.

The problem of selecting a site for excavating was much less difficult in Egypt than in the Tigris-Euphrates Valley. The pharaohs had lived in mud-brick palaces which quickly disintegrated. They saved their splendid engineering skills, as well as their granite, sandstone, and limestone, for mausoleums and temples, the great public works projects of the nation. Much of Egyptian archaeology was in the final analysis merely tomb robbing, and, while tombs gave up evidence of the social and religious customs of the people, they did little to illuminate the political history of the nation. Many of the great tombs were not wholly buried, but were at least partially uncovered for all to see.

The most striking of the ancient monuments were, of course, the pyramids, which housed the remains of rulers (and sometimes lesser lights) of the Old Kingdom and Middle Kingdom. There were large numbers of similar structures in Egypt and Ethiopia, but the greatest concentration lay in a sixty square mile area south of the Delta. Working south, first

we come to the pyramid of Radjedef of Dynasty IV at Abu
Roash, then the great pyramids at El Giza dating to the same
dynasty. Further south near Abusir lay the brick pyramids of
some Dynasty V rulers; then, at Sakkara, the step pyramid of
Zoser and nearby the ruins of some Dynasty V and Dynasty
VI pyramids of Unas, Teti, Pepi, and others. Up to this point,
all of the rulers were associated with the Old Kingdom. Still
farther south at Dashur, Lisht, and Hawara, many of the
rulers of the Middle Kingdom (Dynasty XII) were laid to rest
in pyramids of more modest dimensions. Thereafter the pyramid tomb was abandoned, and royalty was usually buried in
desolate Biban el Moluk, the "Valley of the Tombs of the
Kings," near Thebes well to the south.

The Italian Adventurers in Egypt

The treasure hunters, unaware that tomb robbers had long
since virtually emptied the pyramids, looked upon them as
potential sources of wealth and fame. At the outset, Europeans of Italian background were particularly active. Giovanni B. Caviglia, a former sea captain, found his way to
Egypt after peace had been established and directed his attention to the largest pyramid, that of Khufu, or Cheops, as the
Greeks called him. At one time, this pyramid had been sur-
rounded by a city of the dead where the great nobility lay in
mastabas, and the whole paved area was a sacred place tended
by priests. Caviglia did not locate the proper entrance, which
was forty-five feet up the northern side, but in 1817 he found
a tunnel that had been hacked into the structure by a ninth
century Arab ruler named Mamun. He cleared a passage to
a subterranean chamber and found nothing save a crude sarcophagus too heavy and valueless to be carted away. Subsequently Caviglia searched through some mastabas and explored tombs on the Giza Plateau, and he was still at work
when Vyse appeared on the scene in 1836.

The opening of the second pyramid, that of Khafre (Cephren), in 1818, was the work of another Italian, Giovanni B. Belzoni. Belzoni was a fabulous adventurer who early in life had earned a living as a strong man. In 1803 he came to Britain, married an English woman, and thereafter worked, more or less, in the British interest. In 1818, a French representative in Egypt named Signore Drovetti raised a large sum to blast an opening into the pyramid, but Belzoni anticipated him and found the entrance and the burial chamber. Alas, the Egyptians and Arabs had removed everything but rubbish. Belzoni subsequently acquired a valuable relic, the Philae Obelisk, out from under the nose of Drovetti, and he later became a pioneer European excavator in the Valley of the Tombs of the Kings.

Belzoni published his *Operations and Recent Discoveries within the Pyramids* in 1821 and described his contests with Drovetti to the delight of British readers. He also told of using a battering ram to open a tomb, sitting on mummies (which naturally gave way), and pulling out their hair to establish scientifically whether or not it was real. His daring projects did not bring him much return, and he later went to West Africa, disguised as a native, to improve his fortunes. He died of dysentery near the legendary Timbuctoo in 1823. His faithful wife thereafter tried to make a living with a travelling exhibition which she called the "Egyptian Tomb." Extolling Belzoni's virtues, the *Times* in 1825 added cryptically: "We trust that the friends of Mrs. Belzoni will come forward ere it is too late."

The next of the pyramids to give up its disappointing secrets was the "Step Pyramid" of Zoser of Sakkara. General Henrich Minutoli, a professional soldier of Italian background serving in the Prussian army, opened it in 1819. The upper stories of the pyramid had long since fallen away, and the most attractive feature discovered were the blue glazed walls of the subterranean chambers. The following year, Minutoli led a Prussian expedition to Egypt, and four years later published his *Journey to the Temple of Jupiter Ammon and Upper Egypt,* attractive both to classicists and to students of ancient history.

Searching the Tombs of the Nile Valley

The activities of these Italians prodded popular interest in things Egyptian throughout Europe. Artifacts were eagerly sought. The *Times* in 1821 told of a sale in France conducted by the son of the French representative in Cairo. "Amongst other articles," it noted, "is a great quantity of Papyrus, found in mummy cases. . . ." This was a highly saleable item. During the Old Kingdom, especially Dynasties V and VI, the inscriptions were found on the tomb walls and called the "Pyramid Texts." In the Middle Kingdom they were often painted on mummy cases and called "Coffin Texts," but during the Empire parts of the "Book of the Dead" and other religious writings were copied on papyri and placed in coffins. Dealers in artifacts feverishly searched for them. Other items were also offered on the market. A London sale in 1827 brought £5 10s. for a sepulchral tablet with hieroglyphics; £2 10s. for part of an Egyptian obelisk with hieroglyphics; £2 3s. for an Isis bronze and a bronze wing; and £1 for an embalmed cat.

What impresses one today was the public's almost ghoulish interest in mummies. A mummy and its case was offered for public sale at Plymouth in 1822 to pay the tariff owed on it. It went for £435, an enormous price. But the market did not hold up. The public sale of 1827 noted above brought only £9 11s. 6d. for a mummy and a mere guinea for a mummy's arm. Still, the interest in England was by no means short-lived. In 1842, an official of the British Museum unwrapped a mummy "in the presence of about 200 highly respectable spectators, a great part of whom were ladies, it having been stated that there would be nothing whatever indelicate in the interesting operation." The head fell off during the three-hour exhibition, but such a development was apparently not considered "indelicate."

Fortunately, there was some interest in Egypt beyond mere faddism. In 1828, the Tuscan and French governments sent to Egypt two men who were actually qualified to do archaeological work. One, Jean Francois Champollion, had made his reputation as the translator of hieroglyphics; the other, young Ippolito Rosellini, was a professor of oriental languages at the University of Pisa. Champollion sent back letters to the *Gazette de France* describing the progress of their investigations. On visiting the burial ground near Sakkara he wrote: "This spot, thanks to the rapacious barbarism of dealers in antiquities, is become unfit for any purpose of study." The French philologist died in 1832 leaving Rosellini to publish ten volumes of information regarding their findings during 1832–1840.

The third of the great pyramids at Giza, that of Menkaure (Mycerinos), was not opened until 1837. R. W. Howard Vyse went to Egypt and hired Caviglia to work on the pyramids, but the latter used the money in a search for mummies and was dismissed. Vyse was a career army officer, and his second colleague in the undertaking, John Shae (F.E.) Perring, was an engineer. When they found their way into the pyramid, they were late by many centuries. They discovered a few tablets, a basalt sarcophagus (lost in a wreck on its way to London), and some bones thought to be those of a previous treasure hunter. The most tangible result of this effort was Perring's book *The Pyramids of Egypt* done by a competent engineer. George Steindorff, an American archaeologist, noted years later that Perring had proved the real purpose of the pyramids.

Contemporary writers and speakers had been having a field day foisting on a gullible public strange theories of the pyramids. Some insisted they were the storehouses built by Joseph to store grain in anticipation of the seven lean years; others claimed that they were astronomical observatories; still others said that they contained Divine revelations regarding standards of length, weight and capacity. One Frenchman argued that they were employed "in the cavern mysteries of their

Pagan freemasonry (the oldest in the world, of which the Pyramids were the lodges)." Belzoni had rightly dismissed such theories as absurd; Perring went far toward proving it. The pyramids had temples attached to them and thus seem to have been areas of worship, but the primary purpose was undoubtedly to provide a safe resting place for the pharaohs.

The next expedition of note was also conducted by a competent observer. This was Karl P. Lepsius, who had studied philology at Leipzig and was sent to Egypt by the Prussian government during 1842–1846. He travelled widely in Egypt. At Memphis he located one hundred fifty tombs and made careful copies of such texts as were available. Then he went on to the fabulous Tell el-Amarna but did not begin to discover the wealth of information available there. Perhaps his most important historical contribution was his exploration of the deep south, the Nubia of the ancient Egyptians; there he located Napata (on Gebel Berkel) and Meroë (Begerauie), the capitals of the Ethiopian dynasty, which appeared toward the end of Egyptian history. His important work filled twelve volumes.

A new era of exploration and excavation opened in 1850 when Auguste Mariette came to Egypt. Eight years later the pro-French Said Pasha made Mariette director of the new Cairo Museum, and from that point down to World War I, even after Britain had set up a sort of protectorate in Egypt in 1882, the French determined who would dig in Egypt, where they would dig, and when. Following Mariette, a succession of directors of antiquities exercised authority—Eugène Grébaut, Jacques de Morgan, and Gaston C. C. Maspero—all French, save the last, who was Italian in background. The monopoly was jealously guarded, and Anglo-French relations in Egypt were usually less than cordial. The new era meant that Cairo had first claim on anything found in the country.

Until he died in 1881, Mariette directed all of the continuing excavations—a task far beyond his capacity to perform effectively. Earlier he had discovered a pilgrimage site, the

Serapeum, whose inscriptions were of some historical and cultural value; when he became the virtual dictator, he went on to excavate Sais, Bubastis, and Tanis, sites that were important late in Egyptian history, without finding much of value. The holy city of the Egyptians, called Abydos, where the head of the god Osiris was said to have been buried, yielded up to Mariette thousands of monuments. The temple of Seti I there showed that ruler and his son offering incense to seventy-six previous rulers all the way back to Menes; this became the well-known, if defective, "Abydos List." Mariette also directed operations at Karnak and Medinet Habu near Thebes and at Edfu even farther south. He died in 1881 on the eve of an important discovery; his workers were excavating the pyramids of Pepi I and Merenre near Sakkara, the first to give up inscriptions, or "Pyramid Texts." Measured by the dimensions of his opportunities, Mariette's results were not very impressive. There was little of the scientific archaeologist about him. As Steindorff observed, Mariette "was mostly concerned in obtaining fine specimens for the Museum."

The completion of the excavations of the pyramids at Sakkara, including those of Teti, Unas, and Pepi II, was accomplished by Mariette's fellow countryman and successor at the Department of Antiquities, Gaston C. C. Maspero. The "Pyramid Texts" occupied Maspero's time and challenged his powers as a translator until 1894, when these strange documents, some of them stunningly primitive in their concepts, were finally published.

Maspero was also the central figure in another sensational discovery. From time to time texts from an unknown source had been reaching the antiquities market in Cairo, and Maspero was offered one of them. After some difficulties, he located the tomb robbers, and by a combination of threats and bribes succeeded in inducing one of them to take his assistant, Emil Burgsch, to the source. On a remote hill in the Valley of the Tombs a boulder concealed a forty-foot shaft that led down deep into the mountain. There in the concealed rooms he located the encased mummies of Sequemre, Amenhotep I and his wife, Thothmes II and III, Seti I, and Rameses II and III, which would be like finding the remains of Washington, Jefferson, Lincoln, and others all in one tomb. The pious priest-kings of Dynasty XXI, hoping to prevent the desecration of these former great rulers, had conveyed them from their original tombs to this hiding place. Maspero unwrapped one of the mummies and attempted to photograph its face only to have it disappear in front of the lens. A similar find was made in 1898 in the tomb of Amenhotep II (possibly the only pharaoh before Tutankhamun to be found in his own sarcophagus) where Amenhotep III and several other pharaohs had been concealed.

Maspero went on to other tasks, but he never matched his earlier finds of the Pyramid Texts and the cache of mummies.

The next important French expedition came in 1895, and is called the Mission Amélineau, named for M. E. Amélineau, who received a five year concession to work at Abydos. The royal tombs there predated the pyramids, reaching back to Dynasty I itself. The mission was somewhat marred by a quarrel between its director and Maspero, the former insisting that a skull he had found was that of Osiris and the latter maintaining it was likely to belong to a Dynasty I ruler. At any rate, by the end of the century, the excavators had reached back to the very beginning of Egyptian history in their finds.

Much information relating to all facets of ancient Egyptian life had been recovered by the treasure hunters of the nineteenth century, enough to fill four scholarly volumes called *Ancient Records of Egypt* by James Henry Breasted, published in 1906. The amount of loot sent to European museums was vast, and great obelisks graced Rome, London, Paris, and New York for all to see. The cost of these achievements to history was very large, for the museums were filled with objects whose dates and provenance were alike unknown.

It is true that some progress toward a scientific study of the Egyptian sites had been made, but Petrie could still write regarding Amélineau: "He boasted that he had reduced to chips the pieces of stone vases which he did not care to remove, and burnt up the remains of the woodwork of the First Dynasty in his kitchen."

The most striking example of private enterprise (according to one account, at least) was displayed by a peasant woman, who lived in abject poverty in the village of Tell el-Amarna. While poking around in some ancient rubble in 1887, she discovered a cache of broken tablets filled with cuneiform writing. Realizing that her profits would depend on the number of fragments she had for sale, she broke them further. One hundred sixty pieces eventually found their way to Berlin, eighty-two reached the British Museum, sixty went to Cairo, and a few more were sold to private individuals. These priceless documents were an intimate record of the diplomacy of the fourteenth century B.C. among Egypt, Hatti-land, Mitanni, Babylonia, and Assyria, not to mention the petty rulers and officials in Syria-Palestine, a diplomacy which resembled that of the Old Regime in Europe in the eighteenth century. Those interested in the problems involved in sorting out the shattered and scattered tablets might read Edward F. Campbell, Jr.'s (1944) work on the subject.

Unearthing the Palaces of Assyria and Babylonia

Searching the treasure-house of ancient history that was the Tigris-Euphrates Valley presented more difficult problems than Egypt. The whole area from Constantinople to Persia was technically under the Ottoman ruler, but the farther east and southeast the excavator went, the more feeble became that authority, and in many places he found himself at the mercy of the wandering Bedouin tribes. Technically speaking, he could secure a firman from the Porte granting permission to dig at one or more sites, and until 1881, he could keep

what he found. In actuality he had to deal with semi-
independent local officials and sheiks and a people who
matched the Egyptians in their ability to pilfer relics.

A second difficulty involved the climate. Roughly, there
were three geographical areas. The hilly region formerly controlled by the Assyrians was extremely hot in the summer.
The northern part of the valley, once called Akkad, and the
southern area, once called Sumer, were subject to the overflow
of the lazy Euphrates River between March and July, which
turned some of the mounds into islands to be reached only by
boat and created swamps filled with various types of pests. An
American named John H. Haynes was the first to brave the
climate of the summer months late in the century. "Most of
the time alone, he spent three consecutive years near the
insect-breeding and pestiferous 'Afej swamps," Hermann V.
Hilprecht recalled, "where the temperature in perfect shade
rises to the enormous height of 120 degrees Fahrenheit, and
the stifling sand-storms from the desert often parch the human
skin with the heat of a furnace, while the ever-present insects
bite and sting and buzz through day and night." This was
treasure hunting at its worst.

A third major diffficulty lay in the choice of excavation
sites, which was more complex here than in Egypt. Mounds
were present in abundance in all shapes and sizes and conditions, some resembling mesas, others buttes. "I know of
nothing more exciting or impressive than the first sight of one
of these great Chaldean piles looming in solitary grandeur from
the surrounding plains and marshes," William K. Loftus wrote
in 1849. Other mounds were by no means so solitary. An
observer was much surprised when he viewed the remains of
ancient Babylon in 1811: "Instead of a few insulated mounds,
I found the whole face of the country covered with the ves-
tiges of buildings; in some cases consisting of brick walls sur-
prisingly fresh, in others merely a vast succession of mounds
of rubbish. . . ." Sometimes the Arab name of a mound would
resemble that of an ancient city, which would be of great help

to an excavator, as would the local traditions that clung to some of the mounds. He might also examine the bricks used in contemporary hovels near a mound; if they exhibited cuneiform inscriptions, he could be sure that they were obtained from the local ancient site.

One of these who was much aided by local traditions was Claudius J. Rich, an employee of the East India Company and accomplished linguist, who became the resident of the company at Baghdad. A tradition enabled him to find the general site of ancient Babylon in 1811 and that of Nineveh in 1821. He collected bricks and other artifacts, which he sent back to Britain, and published the *Ruins of Babylon* and *Ancient Nineveh,* which directed public attention to the area, perhaps not so dramatically as the work of Denon, but, in general, the effect was similar. A large number of other explorers followed him, and their observations intensified public interest.

Despite these prods to British curiosity, the first work in the Tigris-Euphrates region was much delayed, and when it began, it was undertaken by a Frenchman. Paul E. Botta, a naturalist and French consular agent at Mosul, used his own money to scratch the top of Kouyunjik, the site of Nineveh, in 1842. Nothing much was uncovered. The following year, one of his workmen induced Botta to try his luck at a mound called Khorsabad and success was almost instantaneous. It proved to be Dur-Sharrukun, the fortress of Sargon, an Assyrian ruler of biblical fame. This news induced the Academy of Paris to offer financial assistance.

Assyria proved to be a goldmine of artifacts, not only cuneiform inscriptions (which could not then be read), but also sensational bas-reliefs, great human-headed bulls, and other animals of the exportable variety dear to museums. Botta continued his work until 1846 and was succeeded by Victor Place at the same site during 1851–1855. "There never has been aroused again such a deep and general interest in the excavation of distant Oriental sites as towards the middle of last century," Hilprecht recalled, "when Sargon's palace rose suddenly out of the ground." This initial impetus to Near Eastern studies given by Botta lasted, however, only until about 1855.

At the moment Britain and France were on better terms than usual, and this happy state of affairs was reflected in the friendship between Botta and Austen Henry Layard, whose interest in the Near East is said to have been engendered by reading the *Arabian Nights*. In 1845 another friend, Stratford Canning, then British ambassador at Constantinople, gave Layard £60 to finance his unauthorized and illegal digging at Kouyunjik, which Botta had abandoned. He worked there and also at a mound called Nimrud, which proved to be ancient Calah, until 1847. His success was instantaneous— more great bulls surfaced, and this time they went to the British Museum rather than to the Louvre. "As a reward for my various services and for my discoveries," Layard wrote, "I was appointed an unpaid attache of Her Majesty's Embassy at Constantinople." Britain was never as generous with her excavators as was France. Layard nevertheless returned for a second investigation during 1849–1851 and displayed considerable literary talent in writing up his discoveries.

In Egypt explorers had discovered many tombs; in the Tigris-Euphrates region, the emphasis was on palaces. At Nineveh, Layard uncovered the palace of Sennacherib, who like Sargon was known from the Bible. Calah (Nimrud) proved an even richer source of such structures: the palace of Ashurnasirpal as restored by Sargon; that of Shalmaneser II, rebuilt by Tiglathpileser II; and those of Adadnirari III, Esarhaddon, and Ashuretililani. The living quarters of some important monarchs from the early ninth century down to the fall of Assyria were well investigated. Identifications here were aided sometimes by the fortunate custom of builders of implanting cylinders in the corners of their structures to identify themselves. "Six feet below the surface, I found a perfect inscribed cylinder," J. E. Taylor wrote concerning investigations at Ur: "The relic was in the solid masonry; it had been placed in a niche formed by the omission of one of the bricks in the layer, and was found standing on end." A neat device, indeed, and one still employed.

Insofar as constructing history was concerned, the great bulls were unimportant compared with other finds of Layard. The Black Obelisk of Shalmaneser II with inscriptions of historical interest turned up in 1846. Then one day Layard entered a small chamber in Sennacherib's palace and found the floor "heaped to the height of a foot or more" with documents, most of them broken, covered with carefully done cuneiform inscriptions on the finest clay. When they were finally read, light flooded into the ancient valley.

Layard left further excavations in the hands of his lieutenant, Hormuzd Rassam, a Chaldaean Christian who had been thoroughly anglicized, but who retained an excellent relationship with his fellow countrymen. The cooperation with France, however, was disturbed by his decision late in 1853 to dig in the area of Kouyunjik reserved for the French. "It was an established rule," Rassam noted, "that whenever one discovered a new palace, no one else could meddle with it, and thus . . . I secured it for England." And England was grateful, for Rassam turned up a cache of tablets that completed the library of Ashurbanipal.

While Botta, Layard, and Rassam were making reputations at Assyrian sites, the large group of mounds—Babil, Kasr, and Amran ibn Ali especially—considered to compose ancient Babylon were not wholly neglected. Layard himself visited the site in 1850 and reported that excavations there would be difficult and very costly.

His discouraging appraisal did not deter two Frenchmen, Fulgence Fresnel, a professional diplomat, and Jules Oppert, an able Assyriologist, who received a 70,000 franc grant from their government to work at Babylon. Despite their qualifications, it turned out to be an ill-fated venture. Oppert believed that ancient Babylon included not only the mounds mentioned above but also El Birs and Tell Ibrahim el-Khalil, which made it fifteen times as large as contemporary Paris. Some members of the expedition fell ill, and the hanging gardens Oppert hoped to find could not be identified. Such artifacts as they collected were accidentally sunk in the Euphrates in 1855. The unsuccessful Frenchmen were succeeded briefly that same year by Sir Henry Rawlinson, a distinguished philologist, whose purpose was to find the Tower of Babel. That historic structure proved elusive, but Rawlinson did determine that El Birs and Tell Ibrahim composed the ancient town of Borsippa, and this reduced considerably the area included in Babylon.

While the work at Babylon was disappointing and unproductive of significant developments, some superficial investigations farther south in the area of ancient Sumer resulted in the identification of certain mounds. The indefatigable Layard spent two weeks in 1851 examining a group of mounds known collectively as Tell Nuffar. This turned out to be Nippur, the most sacred city of the Sumerians. Examined later by American expeditions, the site was to prove extremely productive.

Under the sponsorship of the British Museum, which was seeking exportable artifacts, two other expeditions went to Sumer during this period. William K. Loftus, a geologist by profession, worked sporadically during 1849 and 1854 at Tell Buweriye and Wuswus, part of the huge complex of mounds called Warka, and discovered the town of Uruk (Erech). Very ancient, this town was mentioned in the Sumerian king list as the second (or possibly the third) city-state to hold the kingship after the Flood. Two unrelated mounds at Senkere turned out to be Larsa, or Ellasar as it is called in the Bible, which was one of the important succession states after the fall of Ur III. J. E. Taylor, the British vice consul at Basra, examined two sites in 1854. The mound of Mukayyar, which at certain times of the year could be reached only by boat, was identified as the city of Ur, the birthplace of Abraham and one of the most important city-states of the third millennium B.C. He also turned over a little earth at Abu Shahrain. This proved to be the city of Eridu, the first of all the city-states on the Sumerian king list and obviously a very old settlement.

After 1855, a lengthy period of inactivity set in. For about two decades thereafter excavation in the Tigris-Euphrates Valley came virtually to a standstill. By this time the museums had winged bulls aplenty, and far more cuneiform inscriptions had been discovered than could be deciphered by the small group of Assyriologists then available. Some new development, something sensational, was needed to revive general interest and to start the wheels moving again.

The spark was provided by a young man named George Smith, a self-educated, Bible-centered assistant of Sir Henry Rawlinson. In 1867, Smith was assigned the perplexing problem of sorting out and piecing together the scraps of tablets found in the library of Ashurbanipal. Up to this time the most sensational discovery, insofar as biblical research was concerned, was the Black Obelisk of Shalmaneser II found by Layard in 1846. An Irish scholar, Edward Hincks, read the name of Jehu of Israel and Hazael of Damascus in the inscription on the Obelisk in 1851. Thus, profane history began to supplement the sacred. Young Smith in 1866 had discovered and translated a short inscription of the same Assyrian ruler which also included the name of Jehu. It was this feat, indeed, that had brought him his job. As he patiently sorted out and read the scraps assigned to him, Smith found tablets that contained the names of Pekah and Hosea, kings of Israel, and of Azariah, king of Judah. Public interest quickened. Perhaps the old tablets contained something of importance after all!

In 1872, Smith found a fragment which told of a great flood and of a ship that had been created to survive it. A feverish search turned up some more fragments of the same account, and he found that it was actually part of a large epic consisting of twelve tablets of which the Flood story, still in fragmentary condition, was number eleven. "England did not know how to be calm in the presence of such a discovery as this," Rogers wrote. Smith gave a public lecture on the subject on 3 December 1872 which attracted even William Ewart Gladstone, the pious prime minister himself. Opinion was unanimous—the rest of the story had to be discovered!

The London *Daily Telegraph* advanced the enormous sum of a thousand guineas to the British Museum to finance Smith in a search for the missing portions of the tablet. After some delay in securing the necessary firman from the slow-moving Porte, Smith arrived at Calah in April 1873 to search again through the Ashurbanipal library for the needle in the haystack. The amazing thing is that on 14 May 1873, six weeks after the search began, Smith came up with the first seventeen lines of the story. Insofar as his backer was concerned, the mission was accomplished and Smith had to come home.

Smith managed to return to the site under the sponsorship of the British Museum and worked there until 1874. All told, he discovered some three thousand tablets and parts of tablets, which not only added to the large body of Babylonian literature then accumulating but included documents of great historical importance—among them the chronicle of Agumkagrime, a Kassite ruler; part of the Synchronous History of Assyria and Babylonia (a document drawn up in the time of Ashurbanipal to summarize the boundary disputes between the two countries over an eight hundred year period); and parts of the annals of the last few rulers of Assyria, Sennacherib, Esarhaddon, Ashurbanipal, and Sinsharishkun. Smith returned to the east in 1876 after publishing his findings, where he died of fever at the age of thirty-six. He and his contemporary, Heinrich Schliemann, restored public interest in archaeology.

Responding to demand, the British Museum searched for a replacement for Smith, and waiting in the wings was Hormuzd Rassam ready to make his final performance. He returned to Assyria to excavate a mound called Balawat. His orders were to search for tablets; these he ignored. Ignored also were the terms of his firman and the sentiments of the local population, who resented his digging into a cemetery. Rassam nevertheless vindicated himself by unearthing the bronze panels of Shalmaneser III, the last important discovery to be made in Assyria during the century. Then he moved on to excavate Abu Habba, a two hundred fifty acre mound in Babylonia which proved to be a long-sought town called Sippara, perhaps the oldest northerly site, complete with a temple to the god Shamash. The latter had been restored by the Chaldaean ruler Nabonidus in the sixth century B.C.. As we shall see later, the discovery of his foundation cylinders caused much confusion to later chronologists. All told, Rassam recovered about sixty thousand tablets between 1878 and 1882, and he retired as one of the most successful of the treasure seekers.

The expeditions later in the century, the more important finding their way into Sumer, were better planned, and much longer-lived than those undertaken earlier. The French vice consul at Barsa, Ernest de Sarzec, began operations in 1877 at a great mound called Tello and continued operations there until 1900. This proved to be the important Sumerian city of Lagash, and the documents discovered were little short of sensational in revealing the history and politics of that city-state—the writings of generals, politicians, and even a liberal reformer emerged from the mound. More is known concerning this Sumerian city-state than any other. Strangely, in view of these findings, the Sumerian king list never recorded the kingship as having been in Lagash, thus reducing it to lesser importance than many other city-states.

The first major American attempt to aid in the recovery of the Near Eastern past was sponsored by the University of Pennsylvania. Four expeditions were sent out between 1888 and 1900, the details of which were recounted (with some asperity, as he did not always approve of the leadership) by Hermann V. Hilprecht in his *Explorations in Bible Lands during the 19th Century*. The Americans made an excellent selection—the mound called Nuffar, ancient Nippur, where Layard had briefly trod. The temple to Enlil discovered there

dated to the Agade Dynasty of the third millennium B.C., and
below it was still another thirty feet of artifacts, indicating that
the site was a very old one indeed. The richest discovery was
Tablet Hill, whose documents were gradually recovered over
a lengthy period and proved of enormous historical importance.

Whether the excavations in the Tigris-Euphrates Valley
were as destructive of history as those in Egypt in the nineteenth century is difficult to judge, but they were probably less
so if only because they began later there than in Egypt. Still
the verdict is far from satisfactory. "We have, as yet, no
ceramic record in either Babylonia or Assyria," Archibald H.
Sayce wrote in 1907. "Until very recently there has been no
attempt in either country at scientific excavation. . . . The excavations controlled by the British Museum have . . . been for
the most part destructive rather than scientific; such objects
as were wanted by the Museum were alone sought after. . . ."
On this note the century closes.

Recovering the Cities of Priam and Agamemnon

In the back of the minds of most of the excavators, not to
mention their workmen and assorted government officials,
was the glimmer of gold. Unfortunately for them, many others
in the past had had a similar motivation, and the major treasure hoards had long since been plundered. Small quantities
of gold objects sometimes turned up in the Tigris-Euphrates
Valley, but the possibilities there were never so great as in
Egypt, which in ancient times had exploited the mines of
Nubia. The most notable discovery in Egypt was made by
Jacques de Morgan in 1894 in the vaults of two Middle
Kingdom princesses buried at Dashur. Concealed underground, the hoards there had escaped the notice of previous
gold hunters. They consisted of many objects of female adorn-
ment, semiprecious stones set in gold (ancient Egypt did not
have diamonds and corundum gems), all executed with superb
workmanship.

The archaeologist whose name, rightly or wrongly, has been

linked with gold was the German-born son of a discredited Lutheran pastor, a business man named Heinrich Schliemann. His life was an Horatio Alger tale. Born poor, Schliemann, through temperance, self-denial, hard work, and a gift for languages, amassed a sizeable fortune. When still a youth he became the agent of an indigo firm which tapped the Russian market. By taking advantage of the shortages arising from the blockades of the Crimean and Civil wars and trading on his own, Schliemann was able by 1863 to abandon commercial enterprise in favor of real estate and securities. This left him free to become the leading peripatetic of the period. Mercurial, demanding, vigorous, and sometimes unscrupulous, Schliemann was a cosmopolite in an age of burning nationalism. Settled for years in Russia with a wife he didn't like, he became an American citizen in order to divorce her, then went on to marry a Greek woman and live in her country. His ambiguous citizenship status left Schliemann free to seek diplomatic aid when necessary from many countries.

Like almost all of his educated contemporaries, Schliemann was a devotee of Homer; but, unlike most of them, he believed that the *Iliad* was an accurate historical account of events long past in Greece and western Asia Minor. From descriptions he found in Homer and Strabo, Schliemann believed that Hissarlik Hill was the site of ancient Troy. "From Hissarlik one can also see the Ida," he wrote, "from whose peak Zeus watched over Troy." He secured the site, and— with the aid of an American representative to the Porte—a firman to commence his work. Late in 1871, he secured the services of a railway builder, and they ripped a huge trench through the hill. Progress reports were sent back to British and German newspapers: the discovery of the Great Tower of Ilium, the Pergamus of Troy, the Scaean Gate, and the palace of King Priam. In 1873 Schliemann came on a large cache of gold and silver objects dramatically called "Priam's Treasure," which he quietly spirited out of the country and hid in Greece. The Turkish government quickly brought suit in a Greek court and won. Schliemann paid a fine but kept the treasure.

Under these circumstances, Schliemann found it convenient to transfer the locus of his operations to Greece. There he dug in the mound of Mycenae from whence had come Agamemnon, the enemy of Troy and described by Homer as rich in gold. The Greek government was slow in granting him permission to dig, but finally, in 1876, under pressure from his friends, they granted him leave. "You must know that he eagerly demolishes anything Roman and Greek," an official observer wrote, "in order to lay bare the Pelasgian walls." Through Schliemann's dispatches to the *Times* (London), the public learned of his discovery of the Lion Gate, the Cyclopean houses, and the startling riches of the shaft graves, exceeding those of Troy, called the "Treasury of Atreus."

The restless Schliemann never stopped investigating and attempting to prove the accuracy of Homer. He was at Troy again in 1878–1879, at Orchomenos (another Mycenaean town) where he turned up the "gray Minyan Ware" in 1880–1881, at Troy for a third time in 1882, at Tiryns (another important Mycenaean town) in 1884, and finally back to the scene of his initial triumph in 1889–1890. Late in 1890, Schliemann visited the excavations at Pompeii, collapsed on a street in Naples, and died from an infection.

Even though later in his career as an archaeologist Schliemann employed able assistants, such as Emile Louis Burnouf, Rudolph Virchow, and William Dörpfeld, he could never quite divest himself of the role of the gold hunter, and archaeologists have never ceased to deplore his cavalier methods. His accomplishments beyond stimulating popular interest in archaeology may, indeed, be overlooked amid the chorus of criticism. The fact is that Schliemann added a new Western dimension to the ancient world through his discovery of Troy and brought into focus what is called the Mycenaean Age, the earliest notable culture in the history of Europe. His proof of the historicity of Troy, long regarded as merely the romantic setting for a splendid epic poem, created a new respect among historians for ancient traditions and led inevitably to the rediscovery of the third major factor in early Greek history—the brilliant civilization on the island of Crete.

3

The Progress
of Archaeology

EXACTLY WHEN MODERN archaeology appeared and who should receive credit for bringing it into being are not entirely clear. Many nineteenth century diggers, such as Belzoni, proceeded carefully and conscientiously when handling beautiful objects recovered from the past; on the other hand, Petrie as late as 1927 condemned the methods of the French at Byblos. "The excavation was a piteous sight," he wrote, "the earth cut down through some eight feet of ruin (which needed search layer by layer) and thrown in lumps into trucks to be tipped into the sea." The painstaking type of labor associated with modern archaeology seems to have developed gradually and unevenly from place to place.

Probably the best claim to the fatherhood of modern methodology in the field could be pressed by Sir William M. Flinders Petrie, a British archaeologist who first went to Egypt in 1880 and worked there or in Palestine almost every year until 1931. In 1892 he became a part-time professor at University College, London, and spent the warmer months at teaching and winters at field work. He had almost a quarter century's practical experience behind him when he published *Methods and Aims in Archaeology* (1904).

"In few kinds of work are the results so directly dependent on the personality of the worker as in excavating," he wrote. The qualifications he set for the archaeologist were testing, even severe. "Best of all is the combination of the scholar and the engineer," he stated, "the man of languages and the man of physics and mathematics. . . ." A thorough knowledge of history, surveying, and chemistry were also required of him (or her, as female students often went on his digs). Petrie's archaeologist thus resembled more closely the multi-sided man of the Renaissance than the specialist of the twentieth century.

Petrie's formula for selecting a site was simple enough. He calculated that the mud-brick houses in Egypt disintegrated at a rate that would add twenty inches per century to a mound; in rainy Syria, the addition might be fifty inches. With this in mind, he would examine the pottery sherds on the top of the mound to secure an approximate date for its final occupation. Once this had been established, he would measure the height of the mound, divide by twenty inches, and add the result to the date he had secured from the top. Thus, a fifty-foot mound abandoned in 100 B.C. might go back three thousand years to the beginning of Egyptian history.

While objections might be raised to this method of estimating the age of a mound, none at all have been leveled at his emphasis on pottery. "Pottery is . . . the greatest resource of the archaeologist," he observed. "For variety of form and texture, for decoration, for rapid change, for its quick fall into oblivion, and for its incomparable abundance, it is in every respect the most important material for study, and it constitutes the essential alphabet of archaeology in every land."

An intense study of pottery, its composition, methods of manufacture, and styles, became the basic concern of the new archaeology. Petrie described how he employed his method at Lachish in 1890: "The site was ideal for gaining a first outline of the archaeology. The stream had cut away one side of the mound of ruin sixty feet thick, and I could begin by terracing along each level, and getting out its pottery." In this unusual case, nature had done much of the archaeologist's work for him.

As Petrie terraced the levels of the mound and took out its pottery sherds, he kept a careful record of the sequence of the levels and the styles of pottery found in them. This was "sequence dating." The method did not establish calendar dates for any level of the mound, but if a distinctive style of pottery came to light, say, at level 5 of one mound, and it was found again in, say, level 10 of another mound, it would be assumed that level 5 of the first mound was contemporary with level 10 of the second. Then, if he were lucky, the same type of pottery would be found at a third site which could be dated.

An example of the method was described by Petrie during his excavations at Kahun in Egypt in 1890. The strata in which he worked could be traced by its artifacts to the Middle Kingdom of Egypt, whose dates to some extent were known; but Petrie also discovered there a pottery style which he traced to the far-off Aegean region. Many scholars at the time derided his conclusion. "Suddenly," Petrie wrote, "the Kamares painted pottery turned up in Crete, the Middle Minoan period was defined, and Crete fell into line with Egyptian facts." In other words, the Middle Minoan period at Crete could be considered contemporary with the Egyptian Middle Kingdom because its distinctive pottery was found at Kahun in a Middle Kingdom level.

As a pioneer in the field, Petrie often found his views under strong attack. A Professor Legge read a paper entitled "New Light on Sequence Dating" at a meeting of the Society of Biblical Archaeology in London in 1913. Petrie had discovered some black-topped red pots at Abadiyeh and Hu in Egypt which he assumed were the earliest produced there, only to have Randall MacIver in his Nubian expedition discover that women in that region were still making these pots! Legge called for an abandonment of the whole system of se-

quence dating. Petrie undoubtedly made errors, some of them
even flagrant, in his chronological conclusions, but Legge was
rejected. Petrie's basic approach was sound and still under-
girds archaeology.

Of almost equal importance to archaeology was Petrie's
emphasis on the proper handling and storing of artifacts. Here
some knowledge of chemistry was of great importance. In his
book, Petrie gave careful instructions regarding the cleaning
and care of silver, bronze, copper, and lead artifacts; how to
pack artifacts for shipment; how to dry stone and earthenware
long in the earth; how to open ancient papyrus rolls, and so
on. "The preservation of objects that are found is a necessary
duty of the finder," he admonished. "To disclose things only
to destroy them, when a more skillful or patient worker might
have added them to the world's treasures, is a hideous fault."

Archaeological methodology has made much progress since
Petrie's time and has become ever more time-consuming. The
techniques to be employed, however, must depend upon the
amount of money an expedition has available for any given
project. If funds are available, the technique involves stripping
the mound layer by layer, carefully preserving the information
provided by each layer before (more or less) destroying it
and going down to the next one. Distinguishing these layers
requires no inconsiderable amount of archaeological expertise.
Some mounds are very large, and often funds are limited so
that the diggers must be content with excavating trial trenches
and stratification pits.

Inevitably, twentieth century science has come to the aid
of the archaeologist. Ultraviolet photographs taken from the
air can sometimes spot ancient buildings buried underground.
Even more sophisticated is the use of the space-age mag-
nometer to measure the changes in the earth's magnetic field
due to the presence of underground ruins. Still another aid in
choosing an archaeological site is the phosphate test. An
analysis of the amount of phosphate in a soil sample will
determine whether a given site has ever been inhabited by

humans or animals. The discovery of Swedish scientist Lennart von Post that pollen is almost indestructible has enabled archaeologists to determine the plant life existing when an underground level was at the surface. Still another scientific aid, the carbon dating method, will be discussed later.

Even with all the aids and the accumulation of expertise through the decades, archaeology still offers challenges. One of the recurring difficulties involves "intrusions," pottery or other artifacts that one way or another find their way to a level lower than the time of their production. Sir Charles Leonard Woolley, working at Alalakh, told of finding a type of glazed earthenware at an ancient level. Believing that pottery of this type was not produced until much later, he gave his staff a stiff lecture on being more careful about spotting intrusions. Later, some sherds of the same type were found under some undisturbed brickwork. "I had to give my staff another lecture," he recalled, "to the effect that one mustn't think one knows everything. . . . It was rather humiliating." Later he learned from his friend Cyril John Gadd that the formula for such pottery was known much earlier than had been supposed, and it had been produced in small quantities.

New Techniques and Discoveries in Egypt

Archaeological research in the Near East in the twentieth century has been so intensive that I will do no more than mention certain expeditions of historical importance and apologize to those which have been omitted.

It would be difficult to list here all of Petrie's sites in Egypt. His work at the cemetery at Nakata (1894) and at Badari (1924) aided him in producing his chronology of the prehistoric Egyptian cultures. At Abydos (1899) he gathered important information regarding the Old Kingdom from the rubbish heaps left by the Amélineau expedition. While digging at Thebes (1896) he discovered what is called the "Merenptah Stele." On examining its hieroglyphs, Petrie told a friend: " 'Why, this is Israel,' said I. 'So it is, and won't the reverends be pleased,' was his reply. To the astonishment of the rest of our party I said at dinner that night, 'This stele will be better known in the world than anything else I have found' and so it proved." This was the first mention of Israel discovered in the Middle East. Yes—the reverends and countless others were delighted.

The area south of Egypt proper, which looms large in the history of Dynasty XXV in Egypt, had been explored by Karl P. Lepsius as far back as the 1840s and the ancient capitals at Napata and Meroë discovered. The Harvard-Boston expedition, led by George A. Reisner, excavated a site called Inebruw-Amenemhat and discovered what is called the Kerma culture during 1913–1915. It was of importance from an ethnic standpoint in revealing the distribution of races in the Sudan at a very early date.

Ever since Belzoni's time, the Valley of the Tombs of the Kings had attracted the attention of archaeologists hunting vainly for undisturbed royal burial sites. During 1904–1908 a wealthy American, Theodore M. Davis, sponsored a highly successful series of digs which opened the rifled tombs of Thothmes IV, Amenhotep IV, and Horemheb, the last two of great historical importance. In 1905 they came upon an undisturbed tomb filled with gilded objects, mummy cases, alabaster vases, chairs, and boxes, and even a chariot. This was the resting place of Tuya and Yuya, parents of Queen Tiye, wife of Amenhotep III. "Meanwhile, it had revealed one striking fact," the *Times* (London) observed, "the ostentatious, not to say vulgar, display of wealth which distinguished Egyptian society in the later days of the 18th Dynasty." By 1912 Davis was convinced the treasures of the valley had been exhausted.

Among the skilled archaeologists that Davis employed on his expedition was Howard Carter, a veteran who had previously worked for Petrie and Maspero. He and the fifth earl of Carnarvon received the concession to dig in the valley once Davis had formally abandoned it in 1914. The war prevented any extensive work at that time, but in 1916 Carter learned that some local tomb robbers had located a burial site on a cliff overlooking the valley. He rushed to the place and seized control of it. It turned out to have been built for a queen, Hatshepsut, but she apparently thought the better of it and chose to be buried elsewhere.

Carter and Carnarvon worked their concession every year during 1917–1922, and, in the former's words, they drew a "blank." For what was to be their final effort they chose an area occupied by ancient workmen who had built the tomb of Rameses VI. Digging began on 1 November 1922, and almost immediately a single step was located. This created some excitement, and the diggers rapidly uncovered sixteen steps which led to a sealed door. At this point Carter sent a telegram to Carnarvon in Britain to come to the site post haste. Work was resumed on 25 November 1922. They removed the door and dug through a passageway leading to another sealed door. A hole was pierced in this one, and Carter peered inside. "There are some wonderful objects here," he said. Indeed there were, including a solid gold sarcophagus. No find since the Flood story so stirred the attention of the general public, and the sobriquet of a youthful, unimportant Egyptian pharaoh, "King Tut," became a household word. It was a fitting reward for all of the efforts to locate a relatively intact tomb after a century of disappointments.

Twentieth Century Discoveries in Babylonia and Assyria

Assyria, which had been a treasure house of information and artifacts in the nineteenth century failed to live up to its early promise. Two expeditions there, however, should be noted. In 1903, German archaeologists worked at Ashur (Kalaat Sherghat), the ancient capital of Assyria, and discovered some objects relating to the early history of that country. More important was the expedition of the University of Chicago to Khorsabad (Dur-Sharrukin) during 1932–

1933. They came upon a small clay tablet which proved to be a comprehensive list of the monarchs of Assyria and thus was of first-rate historical importance.

Babylon, perhaps the most fabulous city of ancient times, continued to beckon, but its secrets proved as elusive as contemporary hopes of trade with China. A German expedition led by Robert Koldewey went there in 1899 and worked until 1913. The problem of a site thirteen miles in circumference was enormous, and after all their effort, only half of it had been properly investigated. They located city walls 136 feet thick and an impressive palace of Nebuchadrezzar. What was identified as the hanging gardens was a minor ruin. Some observers identified the temple of Marduk, the chief of the Babylonian gods, with the Tower of Babel, but controversy on the subject continued. By and large, the excavations proved that Sennacherib had done a thorough job in destroying the ancient city in the seventh century B.C.; only small sections of the First Dynasty town remained.

A few discoveries were made in the area of ancient Sumer. Though the Koldewey expedition dug at Fara without sensational results, an expedition sponsored by the University of Chicago in 1903–1904 trenched some mounds known collectively as Bismaya and proved that it was Adab, a city of minor importance. Perhaps the most important finds, other than in the Ur area, continued to be made at Lagash. Gaston Cros in 1903 took up where de Sarzec had left off, and more of the history of this fascinating town was revealed.

Just after World War I, Harry R. R. H. Hall, sponsored by the British Museum, tried his luck at a site some four miles northwest of Ur called Tell el-Ubaid, but his funds were so limited that he could do little more than prove the feasibility of further digging in the area. The University of Pennsylvania came to the financial rescue of the museum, and they jointly sponsored an expedition, headed by Charles Leonard Woolley, which began work in 1922 and continued through most of the decade.

They unearthed a temple at el-Ubaid built by the rulers of the little-known Ur I Dynasty, which revealed the advanced architectural techniques of the Sumerian people; they also found the famous ziggurat, a temple to the god Nannar at Ur, built in brick stages and many times reconstructed. In comparison with Lagash, the Ur site stood virtually mute, and few inscriptions of historical value were discovered. But Woolley was one of the most inspired and imaginative of archaeologists as well as a popular writer, and he could weave historical patterns with a minimum of material at his disposal. Thanks to both his spade and his pen, the Sumerians took on a personality in history.

New Light from the Holy Land and Syria

Nineteenth century interest in biblical history has been stressed here on more than one occasion, and the question naturally arises, Why did the archaeologists not dig in the Holy Land? The answer is that they did, in many places, and that Jerusalem was the major center of their concern.

As early as 1867, the Palestine Exploration Fund sent Sir Charles Warren to Jerusalem with instructions to discover the ancient walls and gates of the city, the Dome of the Rock, the Holy Sepulchre, and many other biblical sites. It was a tall order, more especially because the city was still very much inhabited and in the hands of Moslems who were not particularly interested in other faiths. Warren discovered the foundations of Solomon's Temple and a tunnel leading to the Virgin's Fountain that predated the founding of the Hebrew Kingdom. Filling the rest of the order was left to others, and others came, one after another.

The outlines of the walls of ancient Jerusalem were established, and the Round and Great towers discovered. One of the more important finds was made by Raymond Weill during 1923–1924; he located and excavated the Jebusite Walls breached by David when he took the city. But here, as at Babylon, the results were disappointing. The ancient city turned out to be rather small, and no artifacts of real importance were uncovered. Undoubtedly much of what the excavators would like to have discovered lay many feet below the streets of the busy city.

Elsewhere in Palestine, the diggings were more fruitful. When the French discouraged his work in Egypt, Petrie returned to the Holy Land where he had not worked since digging at Lachish in 1890. In 1927 he located Gerar (Tell Jemmeh), and dated its six levels 1500–460 B.C. on the basis of his Egyptian chronology. The seven hundred types of pottery he found there helped establish clearer sequences for southern Palestine. The following year he worked at Beth-pelet, where he uncovered a mass of Hyksos remains including some scarabs and Philistine artifacts. His last venture was at Tell el-Ajjul, believed by him to have been the original site of Gaza and to have flourished during the Hyksos period. To Petrie, Palestine was "Egypt over-the-border," and his primary interest remained in the land of the pharaohs, which had long claimed Palestine as part of its cultural orbit.

Clarence Stanley Fisher, who had worked at the Israeli capital of Samaria during 1908–1910, was a fairly successful Palestinian archaeologist. Sponsored in 1922 by the University of Pennsylvania, he dug at Beth-shean where Saul had been defeated by the Philistines. The mound was peeled off layer by layer, and two inscriptions of historical interest were uncovered. One, written by the Egyptian Nineteenth Dynasty ruler Seti I, told how he had come to the aid of his vassal ruler at Beth-shean and succored him from an enemy. The second was a stele of Rameses II of the same dynasty. Its inscription seemed to prove that Rameses had used Semitic labor to build his city of Raamses in the Delta, which made him a prime candidate to be the pharaoh of the Oppression whose name is not mentioned in the Bible. Quarrels over the translation, however, greatly dimmed the inscription's value.

No town in Palestine, save for Jerusalem, has attracted so

much scholarly attention and controversy as Jericho. Its importance is two-fold—as a major factor in prehistory and as the site of Israelite entrance into Palestine. To quote Joshua 7:20: "So the people shouted when the priests blew with the trumpets; and it came to pass . . . that the wall fell down flat, so that the people went into the city, every man straight before him, and they took the city." No walls were ever of greater historical importance, and those of Jericho were studied by two expeditions, one during 1930–1936 and a second in the 1952–1958 period. This important controversy will be discussed later in connection with Hebrew history.

Probably the most successful of all Palestinian archaeologists from the standpoint of excavating important sites was Frederick Jones Bliss, who first went to Jerusalem in 1894 under the Palestine Exploration Fund and emerged as the leading American expert on Palestine by the turn of the century. His name is associated with work at Gath (Tell ed-Safi), immortalized by Goliath; the home of the prophet Micah, called Moresheth; and Taanach (Tell Taanak), where Deborah sang; not to mention Ascalon, Gezer, and Beth-shemesh. Bliss also dug at Megiddo (Mutasellim), an historic battle site usually identified with Armageddon, where Revelations 16:16 predicts the final battle between good and evil will one day take place. Bliss uncovered the first cuneiform inscription ever found in Palestine, and the Tanaach Tablets gave up some names of Palestinian rulers. But Palestine as a source of political history has run far behind Syria, where the finds have been little short of sensational.

Byblos, a Phoenician settlement, was excavated by a French expedition under Pierre Montet during 1922–1923. Petrie refused an offer to participate in it and later was highly critical of the methods employed. Montet nevertheless located four tombs of historical importance. Tombs I and II named two Byblian rulers as well as the Egyptians, Amenemhat III and Amenemhat IV. Tomb III was less fruitful, but Tomb IV contained the partial name of still another Byblian ruler. This evidence figured in the famous Smith-Albright controversy, which will be discussed later.

In 1929, Claude Schaeffer led a French expedition to Ugarit near modern Ras Shamra, also in the Phoenician area, and work there has been going on ever since. Schaeffer quickly came across a twelfth century B.C. cuneiform document which he turned over to Charles Virolleaud for study. It was written in Akkadian cuneiform, but employed only twenty-seven signs, suggesting an alphabet. Virolleaud, Hans Bauer, and Edouard Dhorme produced translations of the writing in 1930, and their work was confirmed by the discovery of a Ugaritic schoolboy's A-B-Cs dating to the fourteenth century B.C. A few years later, the same alphabet with its Babylonian syllabic equivalents was unearthed. This provided the key to the large body of Ugaritic literature that has been recovered over the years.

Still another French expedition was led by André Parrot to Mari (Tell Hariri) in 1933 and worked there until 1939. A whole practically unknown kingdom was rediscovered whose history spanned the third and early second millennia B.C., small portions of its history appeared among the twenty thousand documents of the royal library. These documents linked Mari with Assyria and the First Dynasty of Babylon, discoveries of great chronological importance. The success of the expedition led to others at the same site during 1951–1955 and again in the 1960s.

Still another Syrian discovery of outstanding importance occurred during Sir Charles Leonard Woolley's work at Alalakh during 1936–1949. Woolley, a veteran excavator, traced the history of this previously unknown city and its port from earliest times to the twelfth century B.C. Woolley's sequence of pottery styles at Alalakh helped inspire Sidney Smith's monumental revision of early second millennium chronology in 1940. Also discovered was the inscribed Idrimi statue, which recounted some political history in which the little-known Mitannian Kingdom was involved. This was highly interesting because the Hurrian-Mitannian state was known chiefly from Egyptian documents and from the excavations done at Nuzu by the University of Chicago.

Syria has continued to be a treasure house of information. In 1975, an Italian expedition led by Paolo Matthiae and Giovanni Pettinato to Mardikh (Ebla) reported the discovery of a large cache of documents. Ibrum of Ebla seems to have been the contemporary of Sargon of Agade and Pepi I of Egypt's Dynasty VI, synchronizations of enormous importance. Biblical, Syrian, and Assyrian history seem destined to be supplemented by the Ebla finds, and major revisions of late third millennium history may be in prospect.

Some other expeditions are worthy of mention, because they helped clear up the complex political history of Syria in ancient times. Maurice Pezard excavated Kadesh (Tell Nebi Mend) in 1921; it was the site of a major battle and was deeply involved in the mid-second millennium B.C. power struggle. David George Hogarth worked at Carchemish during 1911–1914, a town associated both with the Hurrians and the Hieroglyphic Hittites. Qatna (Tell el Mishrife), once a Hyksos center, was excavated by R. du Mesnil du Buisson in 1924; Arpad (Tell Rif'at) was worked by a Czech expedition in 1924; Til Barsip was excavated by François Thureau-Dangin in 1929 and after; and Danish archaeologist Harald Ingholt worked at Hamath in 1931. All of these sites yielded information in varying amounts. The inscriptions found at Til Barsip enabled Abraham Malamat and others to clarify the history of northern Syria during the eleventh to ninth centuries B.C.

The prominence of the French in the history of Syrian excavations is perhaps no coincidence. France received Syria as a mandate in 1920 and did not completely evacuate the country until 1946. Archaeology followed the flag, and in this case few would deny the effectiveness of the mandates system in promoting the study of ancient history.

Three Forgotten Kingdoms

Of three other little-known kingdoms whose historical existence twentieth century archaeologists illuminated, the first resembled Syria in that it had a national orientation. Prior to 1914, Germany and Turkey became increasingly intimate, becoming allies in the disastrous World War I. German archaeologists followed the diplomats into Turkey and brought to light the kingdom of the Hittites, a major power in the second half of the second millennium B.C.

The Hittites, thanks to the Bible, had never been completely forgotten. Esau married a Hittite woman named Judith, and David, of course, filched the wife of the Hittite Uriah. From the biblical references, which are vague, one would imagine that the Hittites were more or less scattered throughout Syria-Palestine without being concentrated into a single kingdom. The same impression was confirmed when the cuneiform documents found during the nineteenth century were deciphered. The Assyrians noted the existence of a great Hittite state in northern Syria during the first millennium B.C., and Egyptian accounts from the fourteenth and thirteenth centuries B.C. told of battles with the Hittites in the Syrian area. On the basis of this evidence, it seemed that the Hittites lived in Syria and that they employed a script usually called "Hittite Hieroglyphics."

In 1905, Hugo Winckler of Berlin University began explorations around Bogazköy in the bend of an Asia Minor river now called Kizilirmak and earlier known as the Halys. He was not the first to go there; Archibald H. Sayce in 1880 had visited the same area and had discovered some tablets which led him to believe this was the Arzawan Kingdom mentioned in the Amarna correspondence. Winckler accepted this identification of the tablets he found in 1905, and he used his discovery to raise support for two major expeditions during

1906–1907, and 1911–1912. Almost immediately, he came across a thirteenth century B.C. treaty between a Hittite ruler and Rameses II of Egypt which had long been known from Egyptian archives. This was only the beginning. Tablets appeared in abundance until Winckler had a library of ten thousand of them.

Others followed in Winckler's footsteps. H. H. von der Osten and Ignace J. Gelb explored Anatolia in 1933; von der Osten published a chronology of what was now known to have been the Hittite Kingdom the same year. Kurt Bittel conducted excavations during 1931–1939 and returned again in 1952 to continue.

King lists were discovered; so were short narratives of political importance, enough to reconstruct a history of the Hittite Kingdom. The history begins and ends in a cloud of speculation but is fairly definite in between. The rulers of this state called themselves "Hattians," a name adopted from the bulk of the population of the state, who spoke an entirely different language. This led to confusion and controversy, but since 1922 the scholarly world has usually called the rulers "Hittites" and the indigenous population "Proto-Hattians." At any rate, a splendid kingdom had been rediscovered, and its history is still being pieced together.

If the Bible preserved the memory of the Hittites, it was early Greek literature that kept alive a vague memory of a kingdom that had once flourished on the island of Crete. Schliemann had intended to dig there but never quite got around to it, so it remained for Sir Arthur Evans to make the great discovery. Evans first had been a newspaperman and later became keeper of the Ashmolean Museum at Oxford. In the latter capacity he became interested in seal-stones recovered from the Aegean area. In 1893, he purchased some that had been discovered on the island of Crete.

From Homer, Evans learned that the seat of Cretan power had been at Knossos, so he directed his attention there and finally was able to acquire property rights to the site. Evans began excavations in 1899 and continued until World War I interrupted his work. He resumed his labors in 1920 and labored until 1932, publishing his findings over a period of years in the multi-volumed *Palace of Minos at Knossos.* Assisted by the lively imagination of Sir Arthur Evans, perhaps the most attractice civilization in ancient times came to light, one whose material comforts equaled those of eighteenth century Europe. The absence of war scenes on the walls of the palace and the many representations of the Minoans (Cretans) at play gave the impression that Minoans had a carefree existence behind the protective wall of their fleet. Historians talked of the "Sea Kings" of Crete, and the "Thalassocracy" created by them.

Evans hoped to determine the literacy of the Aegean peoples during the second millennium B.C., and in 1901 he distinguished three types of writing at Knossos which he called "Hieroglyphics," "Linear Script of Class A," and "Linear Script of Class B." In *Scripta Minoa* (1909), Evans provided scholars with copious information regarding the Cretan Hieroglyphics, but he failed to make the other types available, and he, himself, was unable to decipher any of them. So the Minoan civilization remained mute.

Unexpected aid came from an American pre-World War II expedition, headed by Carl Blegen, working in southern Greece and elsewhere. Among their finds were the famous "Pylos Tablets" written in the Linear B script and published in 1951. The very next year a British architect named Michael Ventris, using a grid system in his research, announced that the Linear B script had been used to write a Greek dialect. He inspired many believers, but some skeptics declared that the only Greek in the inscriptions was put there by Ventris. In 1957 an American philologist, Cyrus H. Gordon, announced the decoding of the Linear A script which revealed the Akkadian language, but his theory could not be proved, and he himself revised it somewhat the next year.

The third major civilization to be rediscovered in the twentieth century lay hundreds of miles to the east of Crete and well beyond the Tigris-Euphrates Valley itself. In northwestern India, the Indus River flows west-southwest from the Karakorum Range through the states of Punjab and Sind to the Arabian Sea. Near one of its branches, the Ravi River in the Punjab, an ancient archaeological site had long been known; indeed, it had been used as a source of bricks for private dwellings and railway building in the nineteenth century. An Indian archaeologist named Daya Ram Sahni began to work the site in 1921, and he quickly revealed an advanced civilization of venerable origins.

This original site was called Harappa. Farther to the south on the Indus River itself lay Mohenjo Daro ("Mound of the Dead"), whose nature had been less obvious. Another Indian archaeologist, R. D. Banerji, uncovered an equally brilliant culture there in 1922. A third site, Chanu-daro, was discovered in 1931, and by 1960 some sixty sites of what has come to be called the Indus Valley civilization had been uncovered. This ancient culture covered a huge area, about a thousand miles north to south.

Like Crete, it is a mute culture, not because it was illiterate, but because its pictographic script has resisted decipherment. Most of its inscriptions are short and probably would not tell us much even if they could be read. About thirty Indus Valley seals have been found at various sites stretching all the way from Susa to Syria; about a dozen of them came from datable levels in the Near East. In 1932, on the basis of these seals, Cyril John Gadd proposed a chronology for the Indus Valley civlization which placed it between 2350 and 1500 B.C.

The archaeologists of the nineteenth and twentieth centuries had a superlative degree of success in locating the centers of ancient civilizations and in bringing to light an immense mass of material remains that permitted a tentative reconstruction of many aspects of these long-deceased societies. From the standpoint of connected history, the inscriptions they unearthed were all-important—passages on steles, statutes, walls, and especially clay tablets written in dead languages employing unknown scripts. The challenge they presented to the collective European intellect was multi-dimensional, and the breaking of these ancient ciphers is a fascinating story in itself.

4

Breaking
the Ciphers

FORTUNATELY FOR THE rediscovery of the ancient Near East,
the archaeological expeditions of the nineteenth century were
coincidental with the development of the scientific study of languages. Documents shipped to London, Paris and other European cities fell into the hands of a small group of scholars who
immensely enjoyed the challenge of meaningful puzzles.

Modern linguists trace the development of their study, or
science, through a number of stages, the earliest being "grammar," an attempt to establish rules for the correct use of any
given language. This is as old as the Classical Greeks and as
recent as contemporary classrooms. An offshoot of this field,
called "philology," founded in 1777 by Frederick August
Wolf, concerned itself with the critical examination of texts,
ancient and modern. Philology broke the ground for historical linguistics and led, in 1816, to the "comparative philology" of Franz Bopp, a complex attempt to classify languages
in family groups. Later in that century, students of language
began to discover and clarify rules which seem to govern the
evolution of languages (for none are static), and "linguistics"
was born.

The study of languages was centered particularly in Germany, but all of the Western nations contributed to it. The decipherment of the ancient scripts attracted minds of a certain distinctive quality, those that relish anagrams, rebuses, and crossword puzzles, not to mention codes, and such minds are widely dispersed throughout the world.

The Challanges of Egyptian Writing

So it was that the Rosetta Stone almost immediately attracted widespread attention. The lower portion in Greek was read easily and revealed a decree that had been issued in 196 B.C. in honor of Ptolemy V. Above it was the same decree written (as we know now) in demotic Egyptian, a form of writing the Egyptians adopted in the seventh century B.C. The top portion, unfortunately broken, was filled with those hieroglyphs which have been universally admired as a form of art.

The Egyptian portions were written in a dead language employing scripts long since forgotten. But, fortunately for decipherers, a part of contemporary Egyptian population is composed of Copts, Christians whose Bible, based on the Septuagint version and a Greek New Testament dating to the third century A.D., was written in a form of the ancient Egyptian language. While the Copts themselves later adopted the Arabic language, their liturgy was still in ancient Coptic, which could still be pronounced and understood.

Leaving the hieroglyphic portion for later consideration, Silvestre de Sacy, attacked the demotic writing and attempted —by comparing the inscription with the Greek portion already translated—to find names. Although de Sacy was well versed in Coptic and other languages, his major contribution was the discovery that the name of the ruler in the hieroglyphic portion was encased in an oval called a cartouche. The names which he thought he had found in the demotic portion, however, proved to be wrong. A Swedish diplomat and scholar, Johan D. Akerblad, employed the same technique with greater success, located a number of names, and produced something like an alphabet. But the problems were far from solved, and Thomas Young, a British scholar who turned his attention to the stone in 1814, concluded that the hieroglyphic portion would have to be deciphered before, rather than after, the demotic.

Jean Francois Champollion, the Frenchman who was to win everlasting fame as a decipherer, was a youthful prodigy who became a professor of history at Grenoble at the age of nineteen. Well versed in Arabic, Syriac, and Coptic, as well as other languages, Champollion's approach to the problem was thoroughly orthodox; he collected and examined as many specimens of Egyptian writing as he could, not only in hieroglyphics and demotic, but also in an old linear form called hieratic that preserved the general outline of the hieroglyphs.

The work of de Sacy and Akerblad (especially the latter) pointed the way. The key to discovering the phonetic values of the pictures lay in studying how the names of various rulers of Egypt were reproduced. The Rosetta Stone had only one cartouche, which was known (from the Greek portion) to contain the name Ptolemy. To the pictures he found in it Champollion tentatively gave the values p-t-w-l-m-y-s, but how could he prove he was right? To do so he had to find another name with some of the same letters in it. As we have seen, Belzoni had purloined a fine Egyptian monument called the Philae Obelisk which featured two cartouches, one of them spelling out Ptolemy, the other, Cleopatra. Champollion found the letters k-l-e-o-p-t-r-a in this cartouche and showed that three of his previous identifications were apparently correct.

Thereafter he hunted down all the cartouches available (most of them were from the Greco-Roman period of Egyptian history) and names of the Egyptian gods, and by 1824, when he published his *Précis du Système Hiéroglyphique des Anciens Egyptiens,* he had acquired the phonetic values of all of the pictures most commonly used in the system. While the total of such pictures numbered in the hundreds, the constant repetition of a small group of them suggested that the Egyptians had something like an alphabet. He spent the rest of his short life working out the details of Egyptian grammar; this study together with a dictionary was published about a decade after his death in 1832. (Those interested in this fascinating form of writing might consult E. A. Wallis Budge's *First Steps in Egyptian,* an old work, but a very readable one.)

As it turned out, the Egyptians did not create a true alphabet. They had twenty-four consonantal signs, often more than one for the same sound, but no vowels. Vowels were indicated only when the Egyptian scribe had to write a foreign name, like Ptolemy or Cleopatra; their own words were written simply with consonants. So Egyptian vowels can only be surmised, and Egyptologists often simply separate the known consonants with e's in order to make an Egyptian word pronounceable.

This absence of true vowel signs by no means exhausts the complexities of Egyptian writing. Some linguists believe that it went through an evolutionary development. In the first stage, the pictures (called pictographs) meant simply what they depicted—a bird, a man, a snake, and so on. The second stage came when people realized a picture could have a meaning or meanings apart from its pictographic sense. Thus, a picture of the sun might mean heat or light. Used in this manner, the picture is called an ideogram. Some scholars lump both the pictographs and ideograms together and call them logograms. The next step, often called acrophony, was the most important one. Certain Egyptian words, such as "ro" (mouth), "nu" (water), and "deret" (hand) came to be interpreted in terms of their initial consonantal sounds: r, n, and d. These are called phonograms and become letters of an alphabet.

The Egyptians never abandoned their pictographs and ideograms in favor of phonograms, and their inscriptions thus became a robust chaos that included all of them. As an aid to the confused reader, however, they often employed certain signs, called determinatives, placed after a group of signs to suggest what was meant. For example, the name of a god was followed by a picture of a seated, bearded man. Similarly the determinatives assisted in pointing out what was meant when the same signs could be interpreted in different senses. The "mn" sign, followed by a picture of writing gear (indicating an abstract idea), would mean "to abide." If followed by a little bird with its head down, it meant "to be ill." These determinatives were an immense aid to Champollion and Egyptologists thereafter.

It is difficult to escape the conclusion that the Egyptian scribes and priests regarded the hieroglyphs as an art form as well as a means of communication. Hieroglyphs may be read from left to right, from right to left, or from top to bottom— the rule is to read into the faces. Scribes might spell the same word in different ways in the same inscription, or repeat it, or throw in extra signs, sometimes in the wrong place, just to improve the symmetry of their production.

In view of all of these peculiarities, the layman should not be vexed if he finds Egyptologists adopting various spellings for Egyptian names. The same inscription may be translated differently by scholars even at the present time, for not all Egyptian words are known. As Budge pointed out, if a sign is not linked to a determinative and has no equivalent form in Coptic, its meaning must be surmised from the general context of the inscription in which it appears, and this is a subjective determination. All of this is not to underrate, and still less to denigrate, the splendid accomplishment of the nineteenth century philologists, especially Champollion, in this area.

History Begins in Cuneiform

A second puzzle that confronted the early nineteenth-century philologists involved the curious wedge-shaped writing called cuneiform. Its decipherment in some respects was more difficult than the Egyptian hieroglyph problem. On the

other hand, the decipherment of cuneiform proved more re-
warding from an historical point of view.

The story begins geographically in the ruins of Persepolis,
once the capital of the great Persian Empire of the sixth to
fourth centuries B.C. Most educated nineteenth-century Europeans conceived an interest in this empire through their study
of Greek history, and as early as the seventeenth century, Sir
John Chardin copied off some of the cuneiform inscriptions
he found among the ruins. Later travelers did likewise, but it
remained for a German named Carsten Niebuhr, at the cost
of considerable eyestrain, to provide the scholarly world with
a sizeable number of fairly accurate texts from Persepolis
following his visit there in 1765.

Niebuhr noted that the inscriptions generally consisted of
three distinct parts, which he called classes I, II, and III. The
cuneiform became more complex in appearance, culminating
in Class III, a veritable maze. In Class I he counted only
forty-two characters, but his knowledge of languages was so
meager that this fact meant little to him. In 1798, a professor
of oriental languages, Olav G. Tychsen, suggested that the
inscriptions were probably written in three major languages
of the Persian Empire and noted that a recurring diagonal
stroke used in the Class I inscriptions was probably a word
divider. He was right in both cases. Then a Danish scholar
with a taste for puzzles, Frederick Münter, suggested that one
group of wedges in Class I probably meant king, and he isolated the letters a and b. His inspiration apparently gave out
at this point, and he went no further.

The name of a German high school teacher, George F.
Grotefend, is forever associated with the decipherment of
Persian cuneiform, not because he accomplished it, but be-
cause he took the initial steps toward that end and was so ill-
treated by the scholarly establishment of his time. Grotefend,
who was armed with sheer logic rather than a knowledge of
Near Eastern languages, selected two short texts for study.
The cuneiform signs that Münter had identified to mean king

appeared in a number of places in both of them, and Grotefend knew from some recently translated Sassanian (later Persian) inscriptions that a certain form was usually followed: first came the name of the ruler, then came the phrases "great king," and "king of kings." This form seemed to be followed in the two inscriptions he chose to study, but the alphabetic values of the signs for king were unknown.

The first word of the first inscription consisted of seven signs; that of the second inscription had a like number. It seemed probable that these were the names of two kings. Grotefend noted that the name in the first inscription appeared also in the third line of the second with another sign added. Could this mean "son of" the ruler in the first inscription? Probably so. The sign he took to mean "son of" appeared also as the eighth symbol of a name that appeared on the fourth line of the first inscription. This could mean only the father of the ruler mentioned at the outset of the first inscription, so he had three groups of seven symbols each, which presumably spelled out the names of a grandfather, a father, and his son. Who could they be?

The names of the Persian rulers as spelled by the Greeks were well known; the problem was to identify the three men and then locate the original spellings of their names. Some of the Persian names seemed too long; others, too short. Those of Hystaspes, Darius, and Xerxes seemed most probable. The Hebrews had pronounced Darius' name "Daryavesh," so Grotefend read the symbols at the outset of the first inscription as d-a-r-h-e-u-sh. As six of the symbols used in Darius' name appeared also in that of Xerxes, Grotefend used them again and came up with ch-sh-h-a-r-sh-a for Xerxes in the second inscription. Hystaspes caused problems because the name employed only two of his known symbols. He therefore searched some Avestan texts for a probable rendering of the name and finally wrote it as g-o-s-h-t-a-s-p. He believed that these three names thus gave him phonetic renderings of thirteen of the cuneiform signs, and he wrote up his findings and presented them for publication to the Göttingen Academy. His findings—by and large quite accurate—were haughtily rejected by that hidebound establishment because Grotefend was not an orientalist! A friend, however, permitted Grotefend to publish his work in an appendix to a book that appeared in 1815. This splendid decipherer had by then reached the limits of his ability to contribute to the field. Later he attempted without success to decipher the cuneiform of the Class II inscriptions, and his examination of the Class III cuneiform signs resulted only in the tentative identification of several names. The field was left for those with a knowledge of Near Eastern languages.

The Persian language is Indo-European in its family relationship and like other languages changed as the centuries went by. An early form of it was used in the *Avesta*, the sacred book of the Zoroastrians, and this was introduced into Europe by Abraham H. Anquetil-Dupperon. He had become obsessed with oriental studies while in Paris and had enlisted in the army as a private so he could go to India and be near the area of his interest. There he became involved in an Anglo-French war, but he found the opportunity to secure 180 oriental manuscripts from some priests at Surat. He returned to France and published them in 1762. Later in the eighteenth century another Frenchman, Silvestre de Sacy, an Arabic scholar, studied and published inscriptions from the Sassanian period (227–641 A.D.) in a later form of Persian called Pahlavi. These sources provided the vocabulary for ancient Persian much as Coptic had done for ancient Egyptian.

The efforts of three decipherers carried Grotefend's work to a triumphant conclusion. A French authority on the *Avesta*, Eugène Burnouf, searched a list of the satrapies (states) of the old Persian Empire and discovered the values of many more of the cuneiform signs. A friend, a Norwegian named Christian Lassen, carried the work even further and went on to demonstrate that the cuneiform signs represented syllables rather than letters. Sir Henry Rawlinson, an East India Company servant, put on the finishing touches. By 1846, the Class I inscriptions could be read with ease and accuracy. The value of this feat lay not so much in itself as in its consequences. Scholars now had on hand translations of the Class I inscriptions which told them what was to be found in the Class II and Class III versions.

At this point the story focuses on Rawlinson, who had been able to perfect the Class I decipherment because he had a lengthy trilingual inscription from Behistun rock. Near Kermanshah is a cliff some seventeen hundred feet high. About three hundred feet from the ground is a great carving showing a Persian ruler addressing a line of bound captives. Above and below this scene are trilingual inscriptions of the type found at Persepolis. In order to protect the carving from vandals, the sculptors had cut away the rock underneath their creation so that it was most difficult to ascend the cliff to the level of the scene and only a narrow ledge lay below it. While stationed at Kermanshah in 1835, Rawlinson paid daily visits to the site. At no inconsiderable risk to life and limb (he had to balance on a ladder on the narrow ledge), he copied off the Class I and Class II inscriptions.

The Afghan War interrupted his scholarly activities, and not until 1842 was he able to return to Kermanshah to complete his work. Below the Class III portion was nothing but air, and the structure of the rock would have made a mountain goat seek another path. The task was beyond Rawlinson, so he hired a Kurdish boy to do it for him. This intrepid lad scaled the cliff, drove a peg above the inscription, swung across its face on a rope, and drove a peg in the other side, thereby creating a cradle from which he could make "squeezes," imprints on wet paper of the inscription for Rawlinson. This was probably the boldest feat in the history of archaeology.

The words of the Class III inscriptions were not separated by word dividers, and the sight of such a maze of cuneiform signs is enough to make most brains gyrate. The first small step toward decipherment came in 1845 when Isidore de Loewenstein, studying a bilingual Egyptian-cuneiform inscription on a vase, concluded that the latter housed a Semitic language. This discovery was important because the Arabic, Phoenician, Aramaean, and ancient Hebrew languages were widely known and could provide a rich body of vocabulary once the hurdle of the script had been surmounted. Ancient Hebrew in its pointed form even contained vowel signs.

The technique employed was that of Grotefend. A Frenchman named Henri A. de Longperier picked the name Sargon out of the maze. Edward Hincks, an Anglican clergyman whose duties in Ireland left him free time for scholarly pursuits, discovered the name of Nebuchadrezzar of biblical fame. A French scholar, Louis F. J. Caignart de Saulcy, made a close comparison of the Class III text with that of Class I and tentatively identified 120 of the signs. In 1850 the accumulating knowledge of the signs enabled Hincks to demonstrate that they represented syllables, and the following year he found the names of Hazael of Damascus and Jehu of Israel on the Black Obelisk, which made a favorable impression on the general public.

Meanwhile the great decipherer Sir Henry Rawlinson was hard at work on the Behistun inscription he had acquired with such difficulty, and in 1851 he published his translation of it. It caused as much consternation as acclaim. Rawlinson confirmed that the signs represented syllables rather than letters and noted that they might be polyphones, homophones, or ideograms. The first two might be better understood if reduced to English illustrations. The "ough" ending in English has different sounds when used in the words "enough," "dough," and "through"; this is a polyphone. On the other hand, the two letters ending the words "adviser," "advisor," "fakir," and "demur," though spelled differently, are sounded the same and are therefore homophones. It was all very confusing. A cuneiform sign might be sounded in various ways and have different meanings. Several different signs, on the other hand, might be sounded the same way. General skepticism greeted Rawlinson's revelations, and many scholars refused to believe that his method was valid.

The stage was set for one of the more dramatic episodes in the history of decipherment. William H. Fox Talbot, a talented individual known for his development of the first photographic process of 1839, now turned amateur Assyriologist and secured a copy of an untranslated inscription of the Assyrian ruler, Tiglathpileser I. Following the rules established by Rawlinson and Hincks, Talbot made his translation and, in 1857, sent it in a sealed envelope to the Royal Asiatic Society along with a suggestion that other scholars follow the same procedure. Rawlinson, Hincks, and a French scholar, Jules Oppert, accepted the challenge. Talbot and Rawlinson furnished full translations; those of Hincks and Oppert were partial. When a committee of the society opened the envelopes and compared the results, they reported: "The coincidences between the translations, both as to the general sense and verbal rendering, were very remarkable." The scholarly world was now ready to believe that Class III cuneiform could, indeed, be read. In 1860 Oppert published a complete grammar of the language.

Class III of the Behistun inscription was written in Late Babylonian, the final form of a language sometimes divided into Old (ca. 2000 B.C.,) Middle (ca. 1500 B.C.), and New (ca. 1000 B.C.) Babylonian. It was closely related to the language of the cuneiform scripts Botta and Layard had recovered from the Assyrian sites, which likewise had its Old, Middle, and New phases. Both of these dialects were, in turn, related to Old Akkadian, a Semitic language of the third millennium B.C. An enormous body of inscriptions became available as a result of this decipherment, and the fact that Middle Babylonian was the diplomatic language of the period increased the importance of its recovery.

Reading and writing the script was not easy. There were upwards of five thousand signs, and about three hundred fifty were in common use. Most of them stood for syllables in which the vowel might stand either before or after the consonant. Some symbols represented an entire word, a proper name, or an idea. To aid readers in deciding which meaning was intended, Babylonians, like Egyptians, resorted to determinatives which usually stood in front of the sign whose meaning they identified. Nothing approaching an alphabet was created, but separate signs existed for the vowels a, e, i, and u.

The Semitic dialects whose sounds the cuneiform signs were meant to reproduce were among the more stable languages. Their words were commonly composed of three consonants. Semitic dialects are rich in gutteral sounds—ancient Hebrew, for example, has a gutteral h and k, as well as "aleph," "ayin," and possibly another sound, which are not reproduced in Indo-European languages. Edward Hincks, after working on the Class III inscriptions for a time, became aware that these Semitic gutteral sounds were not reproduced very well by the cuneiform signs. He concluded that the writing had been invented by a non-Semitic people whose language was wholly unrelated to Semitic.

This was the origin of what has been called "the Sumerian Problem." In 1853, Rawlinson confirmed Hinck's intuition by discovering cuneiform tablets written in an unknown language which he called Scythian. Meanwhile the library of Ashurbanipal gave up certain bilingual documents of enormous value to the decipherers which related the Assyrian cuneiform signs, grammar, and vocabulary to those of the language of the unknown Scythian people. This discovery proved that this ancient language had survived into the first millennium B.C.

"The learned world was comfortably convinced that none but a Semitic or Aryan people could have been the originators of civilization," A. H. Sayce recalled, "and to assert that the Semites had borrowed their culture from a race which seemed to have affinities with Mongols and Tartars was an outrage upon established prejudices." Hincks suggested that the unknown people might have been a branch of the Indo-European family. Joseph Halevy spent much time and effort trying to show that the unknown language was Semitic cryptographic writing, only to be opposed by Jules Oppert (who named the people Sumerians in 1869) and most of the scholarly community. The publication in 1889 of a bilingual inscription which referred to the "language of Sumer" did much to establish the historicity of the Sumerians.

The Sumerian language was agglutinative. As the word suggests, such languages "glue" words together to form new words, usually without the words involved losing their identity. The process is not unknown in English by any means, as such recent additions to our language as "ongoing," and "input" suggest. Unlike the Semitic languages with their three-consonant words, most Sumerian words consisted of a vowel and a consonant, or a consonant-vowel-consonant; these were glued together in all manner of complex ways. Verbs might be prefixed, suffixed, or even infixed. Various attempts to relate Sumerian to other agglutinative languages, such as Turkic, Finn, and even Bantu, have been wholly unsuccessful, and it was classified by Anthony Arlotto in 1972 as a "language isolate." How it was sounded can be guessed from information in Akkadian and Assyrian sources.

The decipherment of the Persepolis inscriptions and those on Behistun rock thus led to the recovery of the three languages most important in constructing the history of the Tigris-Euphrates Valley—Sumerian, Babylonian, and Assyrian. Such was their importance that they deserve a special section apart from the other ancient languages subsequently discovered.

Class II inscriptions recovered from the Persian ruins presented a long-continuing challenge to decipherers. Niels L. Westergaard was the first to attempt a translation using the same techniques that Grotefend had employed. By isolating certain of the names, he secured phonetic values for some of the signs and concluded that the text was partly alphabetic, partly syllabic. Louis F. J. Caignart de Saulcy noted that the Class II cuneiform resembled more closely that of Class III than Class I, but still considered it to have been the language of the Medes.

The honor of making the first translation fell to Edwin Morris. Rawlinson gave him an accurate copy of the Class II portion of the Behistun inscription, and compared it with the Class I version, now fully and accurately translated. This enabled him in 1852 to publish the Class II translation together with a grammar and commentary. He called the language Scythian, but his work by no means solved the problems involved in the little-known dialect. Sayce in 1874 and 1883 made some provisional translations of inscriptions written in the language, and Franz H. Weissbach in 1890 drew up a comprehensive summary of what was known about the language by that time.

A new phase in the identification of the language opened in 1897 when Jacques J. M. de Morgan began a decade of excavations at Susa, the capital of ancient Elam on the western border of Persia abutting on Babylonia. Slowly facts regarding Elam's history and prehistory were recovered. During the 3000–500 B.C. era Elam was often under the political control of one or another of the states in the valley, which accounted for the similarity between Class II and Class III inscriptions.

Elam presented and still presents many puzzling problems to the linguist and the historian. Among the artifacts recovered at Susa were an early ideographic script and a decimal system of numbers, called "Proto-Elamite." The script has never been deciphered. The possibility exists that the Elamites developed a form of writing on their own and only subsequently adopted that of the valley. When they did so, it was to the practical exclusion of their own language. Almost all of the documents recovered at Susa were written in the Sumerian or Akkadian dialects. George C. Cameron, who compiled a comprehensive Elamite dictionary in the 1930s, was strongly impressed by the differences between written and spoken Elamite and noted that the adopted script, as in the case of the Semites, did not make a proper provision for the sounds of their language. In the 1930s Elamite scholars were still struggling to identify more closely the root meanings of Elamite verbs.

Even before decipherers faced up to the problems of Sumerian and Elamite, still another language appeared on the horizon to test their powers. In 1827, French scholar Frédéric Edouard Schulz was sent by his government into Armenia, north of the Tigris-Euphrates Valley, where, according to tradition, the Assyrian queen Semiramis had constructed some monuments. He explored the region and copied off forty-two cuneiform inscriptions carved in the rocks of the area. Schulz subsequently was murdered by a Kurdish chief who had been acting as his host, but the copies he made were recovered and published in 1840. Other inscriptions in the same language came to light far to the west and east of Lake Van, suggesting that it had once been the capital of a large state north of the valley.

Edward Hincks addressed the problem with some success as early as 1848, but the scholar whose name is forever associated with the decipherment is British churchman and Assyriologist Archibald H. Sayce. In 1882 he laid before the Royal Asiatic Society all the known texts of Vannic, as well as a grammar and vocabulary of the language. "In the decipherment of the Vannic inscriptions," Sayce wrote later, "the ideographs and determinatives which were scattered through them took the place for me of a bilingual text. The determinatives told me what was the nature of the words which followed or preceded them, and so explained the general sense of the passages in which they occurred, while from time to time a phonetically-written word would be replaced in a parallel passage by an ideograph the significance of which was known." He was also much aided by the fact that the Vannic rulers in their inscriptions carefully followed the conventions established by contemporary Assyrian rulers, especially in calling down the wrath of the gods on anyone who destroyed the inscription.

These inscriptions were written by the rulers of the Kingdom of Urartu (or Haldia, as it is sometimes called), which flourished during the first millennium B.C. and often was at war with Assyria. Sayce's work was later perfected, and Vannic inscriptions could be read easily. But this breakthrough was of limited importance because so few inscriptions in the language had been recovered.

After his initial success, Sayce went on to grapple with other unknown languages. Among the documents of the diplomatic correspondence collectively called the "Amarna Letters" were a number written to the king of Egypt by the ruler of Mitanni, whose kingdom was located in northern Mesopotamia and Syria. Following the diplomatic practice of the day, all but one of these letters was written in Babylonian. The odd missive was in a language Sayce called "Mitannian," a seemingly appropriate name. He and Leopold Messerschmidt endeavored to translate it with mixed success. "It is interesting to observe," Sayce wrote, "that in borrowing the script the people of Mitanni had adapted and simplified it in precisely the same way as did the people of Van in after days. Superfluous characters were discarded, a single phonetic value only assigned to each character, and large use made of expressed vowels. In fact, in both Mitannian and Vannic the system of writing begins to approach the alphabetic." As it turned out, the language was Hurrian (Horite in the Bible), named for the basic population of the kingdom; the rulers of the Hurrians were the Mitannians, who were Indo-Europeans. So few examples of the language are extant that Sayce's work has contributed little to ancient history.

Sayce also displayed some interest in the little-known peoples of Asia Minor, especially the Arzawans, whose kingdom also figured in the Amarna correspondence. He wrongly located this kingdom in the bend of the Halys River, and thus

attributed the cuneiform documents found there to the Arzawans. These inscriptions were interesting from a linguistic point
of view since they were in an inflected language, that is, one
like our own in which words are changed to mark case, tense,
number, gender, person and so on. "I can assure the comparative philologist," Sayce wrote confidently in 1907, "that Arzawan is certainly not an Indo-European language. . . ." His
strange reluctance to place the Indo-Europeans on the stage of
history at this time caused him both to miss the Indo-European
character of the Mitannian names and to dismiss the possibility
of the Arzawans, as he wrongly called them, belonging to that
family.

Twentieth-century scholars proved somewhat more flexible
in their views. As we saw earlier, the Germans had carved out
Asia Minor as their particular area for study, and in 1906–
1907 Hugo Winckler recovered a library of documents at
Bogazköy in the Halys region. The documents were an amor-
phous lot; some were written in Sumerian and Babylonian, the
rest were in six other languages. Among the latter, two were
of particular historical interest, being later identified as Hittite
and Luvian. The area also gave up rock carvings in what came
to be termed "Hittite Hieroglyphics."

The unknown language Sayce had studied was written in
Babylonian cuneiform, so the sounding of its syllables was
possible. In a recent study Johannes Lehmann described in
colorful detail how a Czech professor named Bedrich (or
Friedrich) Hrozny stumbled on the truth. In one of the documents, Hrozny found the sentence: "nu [followed by the
Babylonian determinative for "bread"]-an e-iz-za-at-te-ni wa-
a-dar-ma e-ku-ut-te-ni." What does one do with bread? Eat it!
In Old High German the verb "to eat" was "ezzan." What went
along with bread? Why not water? In Old Saxon the word was
spelled "wadar," and so it appeared in the inscription. To
round it out, the "nu" was close to the German "nun," or
"now." So the sentence read (once the unnecessary letters
created by the foreign script were squeezed out): "Now you

shall eat bread and drink water." The Hittite "uga" (I) was close to the Latin "ego"; "eszi" (is) to "est"; "nash" (we) to "nos"; "wi" (wine) to "wine"; "pedan" (place) to "pedon," and so on, as Hrozny compared the Hittite words with cognates drawn from various Indo-European languages.

In 1917 Hrozny triumphantly published *The Language of the Hittites, Its Structure and Membership in the Indo-European Family*. Western Europeans were pleased to learn that some remote members of their family had played a distinguished part in the diplomacy of the mid-second millennium B.C. along with the Mycenaean Greeks. Some German scholars even sought to show that the Hittites settled in Hesse following the collapse of their kingdom!

The so-called Hittite Hieroglyphics, however, remained undeciphered. Some nineteenth-century scholars tried their hands at solving the puzzle. Sayce gave values to some of the pictures, all of which proved to be quite wrong. Hyde Clarke employed the "statistical" method. This involved counting the different signs. If the result were a low number, the writing was assumed to be alphabetic; if it ran around a hundred or so, it would be regarded as syllabic (the five vowels times the twenty consonants); if it reached a high figure, one could be dead certain that pictographs and ideograms were involved. On the basis of his count, Hyde called the Hittite Hieroglyphics alphabetic, but he did not employ his system well—the pictures turned out to be syllabic.

In the absence of a bilingual text, the task of decipherment was brain-breaking. The determinatives had to be selected out, and if one seemed to indicate "city," the symbols around it had to be related to all possible cities. Then other determinatives had to be culled and the symbols around them examined in a similar fashion. A number of scholars established meanings for the symbols one by one, and the most successful was an American, Ignace J. Gelb, who published his third essay on the subject in 1942. By that time, many (though not all) of the inscriptions could be read, and the discovery in

1947 of a bilingual inscription at Karatepe confirmed the soundness of Gelb's work.

The majority of inscriptions in hieroglyphic Hittite, unlike cuneiform Hittite, were centered in northern Syria rather than in Turkey, and were some centuries more recent. The language concealed behind the strange pictures turned out to be a closely related language called Luvian, not Hittite itself. The Luvians, then, were the people so often referred to in Assyrian inscriptions and in the Bible as the Hittites. In proportion to the amount of work involved in its decipherment, the historical contributions of hieroglyphic Hittite were meager; it seems to have been used, according to Maurice Pope, for decorative and advertising purposes instead of as an ordinary means of communication.

The fruits of nineteenth and early twentieth century linguistic scholarship are most impressive. Whenever they had ample materials to work with, scholars cracked the ancient ciphers and rediscovered an enormous amount of information related to the history of the ancient Near East. A few of the scripts, however, resisted them. Among the three types of writing discovered by Sir Arthur Evans at Crete, Cretan hieroglyphs remained undeciphered, and both Linear A and Linear B still caused problems. The writing of the Indus Valley peoples, while widely used, was too limited in quantity for serious work—the longest inscription containing only seventeen letters. Particularly annoying to Classics scholars was the mystery of Etruscan, whose alphabet was well known, but whose inscriptions still defied analysis. Despite such minor failures, linguistics had uncovered a large and ever-increasing body of historical facts. The next problem was to organize them into history.

5

Sothis, Venus, and Chronology

AT THE TURN OF THE century the state of ancient Near Eastern history was disconcerting, frustrating, even maddening. The once-mystifying scripts were then fairly well in hand, and the king lists recovered by the industrious archaeologists could be read with considerable accuracy. But, dates form the skeletal system of history. Without them all of the facts and information that had been gathered formed a disconnected mass. The challenge to discover the dates for the ancient dynasties was undoubtedly the most difficult that has ever confronted the historical community.

The Vexing Problem of Menes

For Egypt, the Turin Papyrus was available, though fragmented by ill-use, and so was the shattered Palermo Stone and lists from Abydos, Sakkara and Karnak, not to mention the king list of Manetho and other sources of the names of Egyptian rulers. Many of these sources agreed that the first ruler of united Egypt bore the name of Menes or one very similar. So the question arose, When did he live? Until the fact had been established, Egyptian history had no starting point.

As far back as 1847, Sir Gardner Wilkinson presented a possible solution to the problem. Josephus had stated that Menes had lived thirteen hundred years before Solomon, but in 1847 it was by no means certain when Solomon had lived. Wilkinson made his own scholarly guesses and came up with 2201 B.C. for Menes, later revised to 2320 B.C., which may have been influenced by Bishop Ussher's date for Solomon.

Few scholars were satisfied with this date, chiefly because so many names of Egyptian rulers were known that it seemed impossible to crowd them all between 2320 B.C. and the sixth century B.C., when fairly firm dates were available. Heinrich Brugsch-Bey, writing in 1902, listed the dates for Menes then advocated by some leading scholars: Boeckh, 5702 B.C.; Unger, 5613 B.C.; Burgsch, 4455 B.C.; Lauth, 4157 B.C.; Lepsius, 3892 B.C., and Bunsen, 3623 B.C. Beyond a general agreement that Menes had lived hundreds of years earlier than Josephus believed, the estimates of the scholars varied so widely as to be utterly useless.

This failure to establish a definite chronology for Egypt had repercussions throughout the Middle East. Egypt had been only one of many important states during the third and second millennia B.C. Others, indeed, had had a much stronger cultural impact on world civilization. What made Egypt so important was that her king lists seemed to be the most comprehensive of any available, and a large number of synchronisms might be made between her rulers and those of other nations. The history of the ancient Near East might hang upon the Egyptian chronology, if one could be firmly established.

The establishment of an Egyptian chronology involved a study of methods of time-reckoning, and the investigation led inevitably into the world of astronomy. The time concepts of day, month, and year, unlike those of hour and week, arise from the structure of the universe and particularly our own solar system, the rotation of the earth on its axis, the rotation of the moon around the earth, and the rotation of the earth around the sun. This simple structure is immensely complicated by the movement of the planets in elliptical patterns and the fact that the sun itself revolves and the whole solar system moves through space. Even with all these masses in movement, various points of reference determine the relationship of the earth to the other heavenly bodies, and astronomers recognize three types of day varying slightly in length, five types of months, and four types of years. Insofar as early man was concerned, the solar day, sidereal year, and lunar month were the ones under observation.

The idea of the day, including both light and darkness, was apparently slow in developing among primitive peoples, and its value in reckoning the passing of the time depended on an ability to count beyond ten fingers. The setting and rising of the sun told early man when to go to bed and when to rise. Imaginative scholars visualize the early inhabitants of the flat unobstructed Tigris-Euphrates Valley and Nile Valley in Egypt studying the horizon at sunrise and sunset. They observed not only the sun but the moon and some of the stars at such times and came to relate what they saw with the seasons and their agricultural pursuits. Probably the earliest time unit beyond the day to be recognized was the lunar month.

The moon, when interposed directly between the sun and the earth, is in darkness for a day or two. Then it appears as a crescent, which continues to expand until the earth is interposed between the moon and the sun, when we see the full moon. After that, the moon wanes and finally disappears from sight. The phases of the moon occupy about 29 days plus 12.5 hours. Some early people attempted to base their calendars on lunar months, but twelve such months occupied only 355 days, and the seasons therefore wandered through the calendar. Lunar calendars could be kept in harmony with the seasons only by adding intercalary weeks at proper intervals.

The early stargazers in their matinal and nocturnal observations of the horizon also noticed certain fixed groups of stars, or constellations. The readily-recognized Pleiades group and the bright star Sothis (Sirius, or the Dog Star) also rose and set. In the process of astral mechanics, the sun in its risings and settings is about four minutes per day slower than the stars, which results during a year in the stars having periods of visibility and invisibility. The Pleiades were watched closely by some early peoples. Martin P. Nilsson in *Primitive Time-reckoning* notes that the natives of Australia believed that this constellation, not the sun, was the source of heat.

Sothis was also carefully watched in some areas. Homer in the *Iliad* wrote uncomplimentary things about the Dog Star, which he thought brought illness and fever. Its heliacal rising in Greece coincided with the fruit harvest in late summer, a hot, unhealthy season. The Egyptians, on the other hand, believed Sothis was a benevolent influence and associated its heliacal rising in July with the inundation of the Nile and the spread of its life-giving waters. What is meant by "heliacal rising"? After a lengthy period during which the star is obscured by the sun, Sothis appears one morning on the horizon and sparkles for a few minutes before the rising sun blots out its light. This brief reappearance after a lengthy absence is called its heliacal rising. The next day it rises four minutes earlier, the third day eight minutes, and so on until six months later it appears at twilight. The time between the heliacal risings of the Dog Star is the Sothic year, which is close to a true year though subject to variations.

Early man thus had his work cut out for him in attempting to devise a stable calendar. The lunar month did not divide evenly into days, and the solar year, which is five hours, forty-eight minutes and some seconds longer than 365 days, could not be divided evenly into either solar days or lunar months.

In this chaotic situation, the Egyptians constructed a calendar which Nilsson called "the greatest intellectual feat in the history of time-reckoning." They cut loose from the lunar month and created twelve artificial months of 30 days each, which were divided into three four-month seasons: the inundation, the planting, and the harvest. From their observations of Sothis, they knew that 360 days did not make a full year, so they added 5 extra (epagomenal) days. This, of course, was not quite enough time, so the 365-days unit of the Egyptians is called a "vague year."

Some of the peculiarities of the Egyptian calendar had long been known from Classical writers. Ludwig Ideler, for example, discussed it in some detail in his *Handbuch der Mathematicischen und Technischen Chronologie,* published in 1825. A whole school of German chronologists, including Wilhelm J. Förster and Hermann K. Usener, appeared late in the nineteenth century and contributed some of the material used by Eduard Meyer in his monumental *Aegyptische Chronologie,* which appeared in 1904.

On the basis of the research of his fellow countrymen, Meyer concluded: "The Sirius [Sothic] year in the fifth, fourth, and third millennia B.C. was almost exactly identical with the Julian year, and since then it has become a little longer. The heliacal rising of Sirius [Sothis] has thus remained on the Julian dates for millennia; in Memphis, for example, where it occurred on the nineteenth of July in the year 4241 B.C., it remained on that date until well beyond the year 1000 B.C., then it moved to 20 July." Meyer therefore assumed that whatever day of the Egyptian calandar that the heliacal rising of Sothis took place was 19 July by the Julian.

The first day of the Egyptian calendar was 1 Thoth, and Meyer believed that the heliacal rising took place on that day in the year that the calendar was adopted. It would continue on that day for four years, then the rising for the next four years would take place on 2 Thoth, the next four on 3 Thoth, and so on through the entire 365-day calendar. After 1,460 Julian years (four times 365), the rising would take place on 1 Thoth again. This was a Sothic cycle. When did the cycles begin—that is, in what years did the heliacal rising and 1 Thoth coincide? A Roman writer named Censorinus (238 A.D.) left a notation by which Meyer calculated that a cycle had begun on 20 July 139 A.D. Using this as the base year, first subtracting 1,460 years and then adding them to the second and third cycles, Meyer estimated the previous cycles had begun on 19 July 1321/20–1318/17 B.C.; 19 July 2781/80–2778/77 B.C.; and 19 July 4241/40–4238/7 B.C.

Because the heliacal rising took place in the Heliopolis-Memphis area of Egypt on 19 July and this was coincidental with the rising also of the Nile, Meyer traced the origins of the calendar to that district. When had it been adopted? As evidence showed that both the wandering calendar and the Sothic year had been known at least as early as Dynasty IV, which he dated 2800 B.C., Meyer wrote: "The Sothic Period 2781/78 is rejected by the leading historical facts. It is proved that the Egyptian calendar must have been adopted in the years 4241/4238 B.C." Thus, the first fixed date in human history is 19 July 4241 B.C.!

How did all this help to establish fixed dates for the rulers of the Egyptian Kingdom? It could do so only if certain notations were discovered that revealed what day on the Egyptian calendar the rising of Sothis actually took place and if the year this occurred could be related to a specific year of a king's reign. Three such notations were available for Senusert III of Dynasty XII and for Amenhotep I and Thothmes III of Dynasty XVIII. Unfortunately, the Thothmes notation was attached to Thothmes' reign but not to a specific year within it.

This writer has never read a satisfactory explanation of exactly how Meyer's system worked. Meyer's own descriptions of it were brief. Relative to the date for Senusert III, he wrote: "In this year the rising of Sothis fell on the sixteenth of Pharmuthi, thus the first of Thoth in the first year of the Tetraeteris fell upon the seventh, and the three following upon the sixth of December, so this date is one of the four years 1882/81–1879/78 B.C." The rising took place on 19 July Julian, and the Egyptian calendar was working backwards toward that date, which it would reach in 1321 B.C. when 1 Thoth and the heliacal rising would again be coincidental. Between 19

July and 7 December (1 Thoth) there were 12.25 days in July; 31 in August; 30 in September; 31 in October; 30 in November; and 6 in December—a total of 140.25 days. Multiply this by four and the total is 561 years. Add the 561 years to 1321, 1320, 1318, and 1317 and we have the dates 1882/81–1879/78 B.C.

The reader might enjoy working out the other two dates. For the year 9 of the reign of Amenhotep I, Meyer calculated that 1 Thoth occurred on 15 September Julian, and his dates were therefore 1550/49–1547/46 B.C. Meyer placed 1 Thoth for the unknown year in Thothmes III's reign on 27 August, and this provided the dates 1474/73–1471/70 B.C.

There was a fourth Sothic date based on a vague story of the high and low water periods of the Nile which dated to the Old Kingdom, probably Dynasty VI. It was calculated that the Egyptian calendar had wandered seventy-five days at the time of this account. This might be multiplied by four for a total of 300 years. Subtract 300 years from 2781 B.C., the start of a Sothic cycle, and the date is 2481 B.C., which would presumably fall within the limits of Dynasty VI.

As Meyer's own dates suggest, there was some uncertainty about the system from the beginning. While 139 A.D. was accepted for the start of a cycle, a coin traced to 143 A.D. fixed the origins of the new cycle in that year, which, if accurate, would have altered all of the dates. There were also a number of other uncertainties that suggested themselves to historians of the period which I shall discuss later.

By and large, the reception of Meyer's work was enthusiastic. A British chronologist noted in the *Times* in 1905: "These dates are calculated by the savants of Germany and by the Chronological and Astronomical Association of London . . . and are reliable according to the science of the time. . . . All history is now placed on a scientific basis." Brave words indeed!

Unfortunately, the system did not provide a date for Menes, so there was still no fixed starting point for the Egyptian chronology. James Henry Breasted of the University of Chicago, who was emerging as the leading American Egyptologist, accepted all of the Sothic dates and created an Egyptian chronology; but the even more eminent Sir William Flinders Petrie established one quite at odds with it. The two might be compared as follows—Breasted's dates are listed first:

Early Dynastic Period (Dynasty I and II)	3400–2980	4326–3838
Old Kingdom (Dynasty III-VI)	2980–2475	3838–3127
1st Intermediate Period (Dynasty VII-XI)	2475–2000	3127–2584
Middle Kingdom (Dynasty XII)	2000–1788	2584–2371
Hyksos Period (Dynasty XIII-XVII)	1788–1580	2371–1583
Empire Period (Dynasty XVIII)	1580–1350	1583–1318

A glance at the starting points and the Dynasty XVIII dates shows that the two Egyptologists were in harmony only during the Empire period.

The Short Chronology, which was the work of Breasted, utilized all four of the Sothic dates and leaned on certain notations in the Turin Papyrus to obtain earlier dates. Breasted believed that he was on absolutely sound ground as far back as 2000 B.C., thanks to the Sothic dates, but he lacked the reign lengths of eighteen monarchs of Dynasties IX and X, so he arbitrarily gave them sixteen years each. The Turin Papyrus noted that 955 years elapsed between the start of Dynasty I and the end of Dynasty VIII, so his dates for all the earlier dynasties were as accurate as the Turin Papyrus might be. Perhaps the most important weakness of the Breasted chronology, aside from his calculations for Dynasties IX and X, was his acceptance of the date 4241 B.C. for the introduction of the calendar. This meant that the calendar had been adopted about eight centuries before the two lands had been united into a single kingdom.

The Long Chronology, which Petrie stoutly defended right down to World War II, utilized the Sothic dates for the Empire period but rejected the earlier ones on the ground that the inscriptions were too garbled. "The rejection of the ancient records, in order to follow a theory of one calendar instead of another," he wrote in 1930, "does not appear reasonable."

He claimed that his chronology was based on "the annals of the early kings, the ancient lists of kings, the inscriptions dated in reigns, biographies and genealogies, epochs fixed by the calendar, the horoscopes, and new moons." Obviously a considerable amount of guesswork and intuition was involved. Where the two chronologies departed widely from each other was in the lengths given to the First Intermediate and Hyksos periods.

These two chronologies by no means exhaust the available outlines of Egyptian history offered by scholars between 1905 and World War II; but, associated as they were with two of the most eminent Egyptologists then active, each chronology acquired its own following. Reasons for uneasiness still remained. Petrie seemed to have stretched the reigns of the rulers of the intermediate periods to unreasonable lengths; on the other hand, the time frame offered by Breasted for the Hyksos period seemed to crowd them. The acceptance by both of the early date for the adoption of the calendar disturbed many scholars who believed that the Egyptians were not yet literate in 4241 B.C. Still another difficulty was raised by astronomer Karl Schoch, the substance of which is obvious from the name of his article "The Length of the Sothic Period Includes 1456 Years" (1928). The eager chronologist who believed that all of the problems had been solved proved to be over-optimistic. Still, the accomplishment of Eduard Meyer should not be underrated. His theory needed refinement, but it was to continue to occupy an honored place in the Egyptian chronological system.

Finding Order in the Babylonian Maze

If the problems presented by the Egyptian chronology are described as severe, those that confronted historians of the Tigris-Euphrates Valley were almost insoluble. Egyptian history, save for certain moments, was the record of one people; the history of the Tigris-Euphrates Valley involved a number of groups. A highly simplified version would include the

Sumer-Akkad period, the Guti conquest, the Ur III period, the Isin-Larsa period, and the First Dynasty of Babylon. Three distinct peoples controlled the political life of the valley during these distant centuries: the Sumerians, whose linguistic affiliation is unknown; the Akkadians, earliest of the Semitic peoples; and the Amorites, Semites who arrived later on the scene.

The history of the Tigris-Euphrates Valley during the third millennium B.C. is further complicated by the existence of many city-states instead of a single kingdom. Some of these, especially Ur, Urak, and Nippur, were Sumerian political units; others, especially Kish and Agade, were Akkadian. The interrelationships of these city-states were fully as complex as those of the states of the Holy Roman Empire.

But the Sumerian memorialists who compiled their king lists late in their history, when there was much more political unity in the valley, assumed that a single kingship had existed from the very beginning and that it had passed from one city to another, usually as a result of armed conflict. The first important fragment of the Sumerian king list was published in 1906. Others became available in 1911, 1914, and 1920–21. These lists were supplemented by those of Berosus.

Pure chance has played no inconsiderable role in determining the historical importance of the nations and rulers of the past. Unless the spade of the archaeologist turns up information about a ruler, he will remain a mere name without historical substance. One of the most fortunate of the ancient rulers in this respect was Hammurabi, a member of the Babylon I Dynasty. Some of his letters were found as well as a law code once thought to have been the earliest in history. Found and published in 1884 was a king list for the whole Babylon I Dynasty, which also provided the reign lengths of the rulers. This dynasty, also termed the Amorite Dynasty of Babylon, achieved more scholarly attention than its political and cultural importance would normally have warranted.

The dynasty provided three centuries of ordered history,

and some of its rulers could be synchronized with those of contemporary dynasties of Isin and Larsa, whose kings were known from the Louvre Prism and the Yale List. Most of the reign lengths of the Larsa rulers were available, and the earliest rulers of these two city-states were known to have been contemporaries of the last ruler of the Ur III Dynasty, whose kings and reigns were recorded on the Sumerian lists. Thus a continuous history could be traced back with some reliability through the Ur III Dynasty. If the dates of Babylon I could be established in terms of the Christian calendar, half a millennium of history could be placed accurately in time.

In the late nineteenth century, it seemed that the friendly hand of an ancient ruler had extended across twenty-five centuries to aid modern scholars in dating the Sumerian king lists. Nabonidus, a Chaldaean monarch of the sixth century B.C., spent much time digging up and refurbishing old temples. On one of his tablets he boasted of locating the foundations of a temple built by Naram Sin of Agade "which for thirty-two hundred years no previous king had seen." If Naram Sin lived thirty-two hundred years before Nabonidus, his date would be about 3750 B.C. This ancient archaeologist also provided a 2080 B.C. date for Hammurabi.

Who would quarrel with the conclusions of a ruler who had lived so much nearer to Naram Sin's time? But the dates presented a problem. Between the Agade Dynasty and the Ur III dynasty were only twenty-seven rulers, some of whom obviously reigned for brief periods; there were five rulers for Ur III and fourteen for the Larsa Dynasty down to the time of Hammurabi. Thus, forty-six rulers had to be stretched over a period from 3650 B.C. (when the Agade Dynasty presumably ended) to 2080 B.C., the time of Hammurabi. Each would have had about a thirty-five year reign. "Over this date there rages a ceaseless controversy," Robert W. Rogers wrote in 1900. "Positive proof on either one side or the other has not yet come to light. . . ." But Rogers nevertheless accepted Nabonidus' date, and traced Sumerian history as far back as 4500 B.C. The eminent cuneiformist Archibald H. Sayce, writing in 1907, likewise approved this Long Chronology.

On the other hand, German scholar Hugo Winckler treated Nabonidus (Nabuna'id) with contempt. "When Nabuna'id ... found an inscription of Sargon's son, Naram Sin," he wrote in 1907, "and appealed to the scholars of his court for information as to its age, they had not the historical data at hand to make a correct computation." This haughty authority, who wrote as if he had been present at the time, rejected the date for Naram Sin as too early, then turned around and gave short shrift to the one for Hammurabi because it was too recent! For the latter, he offered 2267–2213 B.C. instead.

The scholarly world was still divided after Nabonidus' dates were found. Just as Egyptian scholars had turned to Egyptian calendars for aid, scholars did likewise in confronting the problems of Babylonia. The initial discoveries were far from encouraging. During the third millennium B.C., each of the city-states of Sumer-Akkad had its own names for the months, and there was no standardization until Babylon I. Only gradually did the details emerge.

The Babylonian new year was marked by a new moon, and the months thereafter were measured new moon to new moon. A lunar calendar such as this quickly fell out of harmony with the solar year, and the Babylonians, who were enthusiastic stargazers, learned how to correct it through observations of the Pleiades, whose heliacal risings measured the year with accuracy. Once this became known, the Babylonians harmonized the lunar calendar with the sidereal year by injecting extra days into it. This seems to have been done somewhat haphazardly by the rulers and astronomers of Babylon I, without the establishment of a fixed intercalary cycle. Thus, there was nothing about the Babylonian calendar which would permit calculations such as Meyer made for Egypt.

Fortunately, however, the science of astronomy did not fail completely in this area. Sir Austen Layard in 1850 had recovered a document from Ashurbanipal's library which was translated and published two decades later by Sir Henry Rawlinson and George Smith under the title "Tablet of Movements of the Planet Venus and their Influences." While the document attracted immediate interest, its significance remained obscure.

Venus moves in a smaller orbit than the earth and always appears in the same direction as the sun, sometimes to the right and sometimes to the left of it. Its cycle has four phases: the evening star visible after sunset, a period of invisibility when obscured by the sun, the morning star visible before sunrise, then a second period of invisibility. The average duration (synodic period) of these phases is 584 days, but the lengths of the individual phases may vary. What is called the Venus cycle takes approximately eight years, the length of time required for Venus to return to the same starting point in the solar year and lunar month. The return is not precise. Venus arrives 2.5 days earlier in the solar year and 4 days earlier in the lunar month when a cycle is completed. The Babylonians made observations of these interesting habits of Venus and recorded them on the Venus Tablet published by Smith and Rawlinson.

For a long time, the value of the tablets lay unrecognized. Then, in 1912, Franz Xaver Kugler, S. J., a cuneiformist with a mathematical bent, published his "Die ältesten Venus-Tafeln und das Alter der 1 Dynastie von Babel" in *Sternkunde und Sterndienst in Babel.* Kugler showed that the tablets were divided into three parts, which he labeled A, B, and A_1, and that they recorded the Babylonian dates when Venus disappeared in the east, the duration of its invisibility in months and days, the dates when it reappeared in the west, the dates when it disappeared in the west, the duration of its invisibility, and the dates when it reappeared in the east—all over a twenty-one-year period. How could that period be placed in time?

Kugler discovered that line 8 in part A, and line 21 in A_1

bore the regal date formula called the "year of the Golden
Throne." Let Kugler himself describe his process. "Such
formulae for the designation of a precise year we find both in
the Old Babylonian [Sumer-Akkad] period, and under Dynasty I of Babylon. With the appearance of the Kassite
Dynasty this form of dating was abandoned; from then on the
regnal years provided the dates. Thus, we have established a
lower boundary for the period to which the year we are seeking belongs. We can also establish an upper boundary. In both
Document A and in A_1 we find a II Elulu. As we have seen
above, this was first introduced by Hammurabi, and indeed,
during the second half of his reign. Thereafter we must scruti-
nize the known year formulae from that point in time to the
end of Dynasty I. And from this process the fact arises that
Year VIII of Ammi-zaduga is that of the year formula noted
above." Since then the tablet has been named for Ammi-
zaduga.

The twenty-one years of observations, though marred (as
Kugler pointed out) by an occasional error, formed a pattern
distinct enough to be identified in time but one that was
subject to repetitions at irregular intervals. He went on to
translate the Babylonian dates on the tablet in terms of the
Julian calendar and to select from a number of possibilities
the Julian years which seemed most appropriate for the reign
of Ammi-zaduga. The pattern fit the years 1977–1957 B.C.,
and, the regnal years of the rulers preceding and succeeding
Ammi-zaduga being known, he was able to date Hammurabi
2123–2081 B.C. (close to the Nabonidus date) and the whole
dynasty 2225–1926 B.C.

For the first time, a segment of the Tigris-Euphrates chronology had been placed on a rational, even scientific, basis!
Kugler's study won instant acclaim, and his basic approach
was almost universally accepted. But, the weakness of the
chronological conclusions to which it led lay in the fact that
the observations could be fitted into other periods and be
sound from an astronomical point of view. In 1913 Eduard

Meyer suggested that Kugler's chronology did not synchronize very well with the Assyrian king list and therefore might have to be revised. Other scholars made similar observations, and Kugler himself in 1922 admitted that his dating of Babylon I might have to be pushed downward perhaps a century and a half or more.

The uncertainty surrounding Kugler's conclusions led John K. Fotheringham and astronomer Karl Schoch to make a further study of the tablets. Schoch attacked the problems involved in the Babylonian dates with vigor and produced a table which permitted the rapid conversion of such dates into Julian calendar dates which was accurate 80 percent of the time. It has continued to be used by chronologists. But the collaboration fell short of success when he and Fotheringham failed to agree on some of the dates.

An unusual format was employed in *The Venus Tablets of Ammi-zaduga,* published in 1928. Schoch's tables were in the back, and some chapters were written by Fotheringham, others by Stephen H. Langdon. The lengthy chronology from Sumerian times down through the Chaldaean period was the work of Langdon. In it, Naram Sin was moved all the way up to 2671–2634 B.C., and Hammurabi was dated 2067–2025 B.C. Despite these revisions, it can hardly be called a "short chronology" because the second dynasty of Sumer-Akkad, Uruk I, was moved all the way back to 4500 B.C., and its predecessor, Kish I, while undated, was assumed to have begun even earlier.

One of the strongest dissenters was Sidney Smith, who at that time was impressed by the Assyrian king lists then available. He could not synchronize these lists with Langdon's date for Hammurabi. "If the astronomical authorities finally agree that the Amorite Dynasty ruled from 2170–1871," he wrote, "then the evidence of the late chroniclers not only concerning the Amorite Dynasty but also the previous period, so far as synchronisms are concerned, must be abandoned as worthless, and the historian's task will be almost impossible." Smith

seems to have had a strong intuition that Hammurabi must
be moved forward, but at the moment he was unable to prove
his case.

The last major attempt to create an acceptable chronology
for the Tigris-Euphrates Valley prior to World War II was the
work of Thorkild Jacobsen of the University of Chicago. His
major source for the third millennium was the Weld-Blundell
Prism, also known as the Larsa List, which had been published by Langdon in 1923 and which listed the rulers of
Sumer-Akkad (with minor gaps) from the period before the
Flood down through Sin-magir of the Isin Dynasty. But he
had on hand more than a dozen other fragmentary king lists,
which, happily, generally agreed with one another.

Jacobsen accepted the Langdon dates for Babylon I, which
were fortified with a Venus cycle, and employed two lunar
eclipses further back in time, one to end the Ur III Dynasty
in 2283 B.C., the other to foretell the fall of the Guti Dynasty
in 2403 B.C. But Jacobsen's contribution was not so much at
the end of the Sumer-Akkad-Isin-Larsa-Babylon I sequence
as during the earliest phases, which Langdon and everyone
else had left in a highly chaotic state.

The Sumerian king list noted that in the beginning the kingship was lowered from heaven to Eridu. At this moment historians are treading on the very boundary of ancient history,
and they are confronted with a large number of names of
rulers and cities who obviously flourished at the beginning of
civilization in the Tigris-Euphrates Valley. The reigns of the
kings are numbered in thousands of years, but simply because
their longevity is so grossly exaggerated is no reason to reject
their historicity. Still, there is little that can be done with them
in the way of constructing a chronology.

The list continues: "The Flood swept thereover. After the
Flood had swept thereover, when the kingship was lowered
from heaven, the kingship was in Kish." Some rulers thereafter
still have mythical reigns, and it is only at the end of the
Uruk Dynasty, the second (or, perhaps, the third) on the

list, that the reign lengths became believable. When the reign lengths were unknown, or badly exaggerated, Jacobsen allowed twenty years for each ruler, unless he was followed by a son, which suggested political stability; in such cases he allowed thirty years for the reigns. Using this technique and overlapping some of the dynasties, Jacobsen established the date 3111 B.C. for Kish I, the first dynasty after the Flood. While open to criticism, the system at least brought the early history of the Tigris-Euphrates Valley into focus.

As we arrive at World War II, a retrospective look at what the century before had accomplished might be in order. Vast quantities of relics of the past had been recovered, languages long dead had been deciphered, and twenty-five centuries or more of human history was well along the road toward reconstruction—all this by a comparatively small body of scholars, usually unknown to the general public, whose chief motivations stemmed from meeting the intellectual challenges of the complex problems presented to them and winning the respect, even occasionally the praise, of their fellow workers. The boundaries of history had been pushed far back, and strong, general outlines had been drawn. After the war, the ranks of scholars were enlarged, and many more fine minds were recruited to aid in the massive task of filling in the details.

6

The Progress of Chronology

IN 1948, WHEN AMERICAN scientist Willard F. Libby announced the discovery of the Carbon-14 (C-14) method of dating organic remains, chronologists dealing with ancient history were excited and elated. But hope turned to doubt and finally to the conviction that the method wanted considerable refinement before it could be trusted for exact dating purposes.

The Emerging Structure of
Early Egyptian History

Chronologists of the past several decades have been forced to carry on much as they did before—synchronizing names found on the various king lists, working in the scanty astronomical information available, and deriving rough dates from pottery sequences and the estimated longevity of the generations. The failure of the C-14 method merely spurred chronologists on to greater efforts, and some of the most fascinating debates in the history of ancient history have arisen during this period.

The problem of Menes has still not been solved to every-

one's satisfaction. Shortly after World War II, Alexander
Scharff attempted to revise the date for Menes downward because the Egyptian archaeological evidence for this period
resembled that of the Jemdet Nasr period in Babylonia,
thought to have occurred sometime after 3000 B.C. William
F. Albright, Hanns Stock, Raymond Weill, and others moved
Menes into the 2900–2800 B.C. area, but most Egyptologists
were not convinced. The early third millennium B.C. in the
Tigris-Euphrates Valley is much more obscure than that in
Egypt, and to use its conjectural dates to revise the Egyptian
chronology was like having the blind lead the halt.

A rather roundabout method is generally employed to date
Menes today. Most historians agree that Dynasty XII began
in 1991 B.C. The Turin Papyrus noted that 955 years passed
from the beginning of Dynasty I through Dynasty VIII; it also
gave 143 years to Dynasty XI. It is known that Dynasties IX
and X were generally contemporary with Dynasty XI. So 1991,
143, and 955 years are added together for a total of 3089 B.C.
If a few extra years are allowed for IX and X, the result is 3100
B.C. or if one deducts the reigns of certain kings who did not
rule the whole country, it might be as low as 3000 B.C. (Jürgen
von Beckerath desribed this system in an article published in
1962 for those who may be interested in the details.)

This brings us to 1991 B.C., the opening of the Middle
Kingdom and the date that makes possible the above chronology of the Old Kingdom. This was the work of two eminent
scholars, William F. Edgerton and Richard A. Parker. In an
article published in 1942, Edgerton examined in detail the
Sothic date for Senusert III derived from the El Lahun temple
register, particularly with regard to the geographical point
from which the observation was made. As this was uncertain,
Edgerton had to construct mathematical equations which took
into account that the date of the heliacal rising would vary
slightly according to the horizon where the rising took place,
and he established the date 1870 B.C. ± 6 years. While he

was aware of the so-called El Lahun Calendar, actually a work schedule of Egyptian priests, he could not use it to substantiate his Sothic date because he could not link it to any specific ruler or date.

The investigation was continued by Richard A. Parker, whose results were published in his monumental *The Calendars of Ancient Egypt* (1950). The two columns of the El Lahun calendar seemed to provide sequences of lunar observations together with Egyptian calendar dates, and it was necessary to attach these sequences to a definite period of time in the Julian calendar. Parker traced the sequence to the years 1813–1812 B.C. of the reign of Amenemhat III, and these dates, together with some other lunar observations and the Sothic date calculated by Edgerton, permitted Parker to work out a chronology for Dynasty XII between 1991–1786 B.C.

Parker's exact dating of the Middle Kingdom was not seriously attacked for two decades. Then, in 1970, John G. Read found two specific faults with it. He asserted that the Egyptian lunar month began in the evening instead of the morning as Parker had claimed and that the Illahun calendar should be traced to the reign of Ahmose I of Dynasty XVIII rather than Amenemhat III. Parker replied in an article of the same year. Many technical points were involved, but perhaps the strongest rebuttal was that the cache of documents from which the Kahun Papyrus and Illahun calendar were taken came from Dynasty XII or Dynasty XIII at the latest. While imperfect in certain details, the Parker system survived and continues to be the chronological anchor for early Egyptian history.

The dynasties following the end of the Middle Kingdom (Dynasty XII), called Dynasties XIII–XVII, continued to give trouble. The Turin Papyrus provides more than a hundred rulers for these five dynasties who must be crowded into two centuries! While Egypt was invaded once or twice by the Hyksos of Syria-Palestine and many of the rulers and dynasties were obviously contemporary rather than successive, there is still a large number of rulers to accommodate.

Five dynasties must be inserted between Parker's date for the end of Dynasty XII—1786 B.C.—and 1558 B.C., when the first ruler of Dynasty XVIII, Ahmose I, came to the throne. The second date was established in a roundabout fashion. Ludwig Borchardt, in 1935, fixed the year I of the reign of Thothmes III in 1490 B.C., and later Michael B. Rowton fortified the theory through a lunar observation in the fifty-second year of Thothmes III's reign. Three rulers— Thothmes II, Thothmes I, and Amenhotep I—reigned between Ahmose I and Thothmes III; so, using 1490 B.C. as the base, their reigns were added to the reign of Ahmose himself, and the beginning of the Dynasty was established.

Some uncertainty arises because the reign length of Thothmes II is uncertain. A detailed study of the problem was offered in 1967 by a Canadian authority, Donald B. Redford, in his "Chronology of the Egyptian Eighteenth Dynasty." Redford set the reign length of Thothmes II at ten years, made some adjustments in those of Thothmes I and Amenhotep I, and provided a March 1558 B.C. to July 1533 B.C. reign for Ahmose I. Dynasty XVIII as a whole was dated 1558–1303 B.C.

If we follow the Redford chronology, the five dynasties are permitted about two decades less than if a longer chronology is employed. It is generally agreed that Dynasties XIII, XIV, and XVII are native Egyptian dynasties and that Dynasties XV and XVI belong to the Hyksos. Manetho described a savage invasion of Egypt by the Hyksos; more recently the conquest is visualized in less dramatic terms. It is generally agreed that the Hyksos bore mostly Semitic names, but some authorities find a Hurrian or even Indo-European strain among them. Those interested might consult John Van Seters, *The Hyksos: A New Investigation* (1966).

The millions of Americans who have viewed the treasures

of "King Tut" (Tutankhamun), the twelfth ruler of Dynasty XVIII, and have attempted to learn more about him from works dealing with the so-called Amarna Age, are likely to have encountered chronological difficulties. Variations in the reign lengths of the Dynasty XVIII rulers are common. Johannes Lehmann (1975), viewing the situation from the standpoint of Hittite chronology, noted that 1358, 1344, and 1338 B.C. are all possible dates for the death of Tut. Donald B. Redford is associated with the last of these options. Cyril Aldred, in articles published in 1957 and 1959, discussed some of the vexing problems involved in the chronology of the Amarna Age.

The strength of the Egyptian chronology lies in the fact that it has been hammered out in a splendidly chaotic manner through statements of theory, objections, and rebuttals. For some time the dating of Dynasty XIX seemed to be well established, and its most famous ruler, Rameses II, was placed on the throne in 1290 B.C. Then, in 1960, Michael B. Rowton, after studying synchronisms among the Egyptian, Babylonian, Assyrian, and Hittite chronologies, concluded that Rameses II came to the throne somewhat earlier, probably in 1304 B.C. His theory received support from James R. Harris in 1968. Harris showed that an Egyptian workman named Mininiwy had been active during the year 7 of Horemheb, the last ruler of Dynasty XVIII, had lived through the reigns of Rameses I and Seti I, and was chief of police in year 16 of Rameses II. This suggested that the reigns of the kings involved should be reduced to their minimum possible lengths, and Harris concluded 1304 B.C. would fit the situation while 1290 B.C. would not. The latter date has continued to survive.

The end of Dynasty XIX, which peters out with the names Rameses Siptah, Merenptah Siptah, and Twosre, has always been more obscure than its beginning. In 1954 Sir Alan Gardiner worked out a chronology showing all three at the end of the dynasty, only to encounter one of those mystifyingly illogical situations in history for which we may never know the reason. When further evidence came to light he corrected his mistakes in an article amusingly entitled "Only One King Siptah and Twosre Not His Wife." Indeed, she was more likely his mother.

Still another figure intrudes into the picture at the end of Dynasty XIX—a Syrian called Irsu, or Bay. In 1954, Abraham Malamat published the theory that Irsu might be the Cushan Rishathaim mentioned in Judges 3:8-10 who created a short-lived empire of fairly wide dimensions which included the Israelites for an eight-year period.

Dynasty XX began, according to Gardiner and Cyril Aldred, in 1184 B.C.; other scholars prefer 1195 B.C. This undistinguished dynasty produced only one ruler of note, Rameses III. In his year 8, Egypt was attacked by the "P-l-s-t," better known to us as the Philistines, who were beaten off and then settled on the shores of Palestine, there to threaten the Israelites. A curious twilight of decadence, sometimes dramatized by historians such as Oswald Spengler, now settled over the Nile Valley.

About 1094 B.C., the priest-kings of Dynasty XXI took over a people deep in slumber. The only ruler worthy of mention comes toward the last of the line, one Si-Amen (978–959 B.C.) "And Solomon made affinity with Pharaoh king of Egypt, and took Pharaoh's daughter, and brought her into the city of David," to quote I Kings 3:1. In the days of their glory, the Egyptian rulers had accepted the daughters of foreign kings for marriage purposes, but never sent one of their own daughters abroad. Times had changed. The kingdom of Egypt's former Hebrew serfs was stronger now than Egypt.

We thus have a fairly connected and dated history of Egypt from 3100 B.C. down through the tenth century B.C. In going through the account, the reader might wonder what happened to all the Sothic dates that once seemed to undergird the system. The high-level/low-level Nile date of 2481 B.C. for Dynasty VI has been abandoned as too indefinite. The date of Senusert III, on the other hand, is a bulwark of Parker's dating of the Middle Kingdom. The difficulty surrounding the Sothic date for Amenhotep I of Dynasty XVIII lies in the fact that no one knows in which city in Egypt the observation was made, and the year could vary considerably along with the location. The Sothic date for Thothmes III falls within his reign in all of the chronologies, but it is not linked to a particular regnal year.

In 1966, Oliver R. Gurney and others asked M. F. Ingham to establish the exact lengths of the Sothic cycles as observed from Memphis, which, because of the precession of the equinoxes, are not constant. Ingham's article of 1967 presented two sets of dates for the beginning of the cycles: 4226 (4226) B.C.; 2768 (2770) B.C.; 1312 (1316) B.C.; 141 (136) A.D., and 1591 (1585) A.D. The uncertainty arises from the possibility that the angle *arcus visionis* may have changed slightly over the centuries. Ingham noted that the Sothic year gradually shortened down to 970 A.D., after which it lengthened again. Thus, some exact information is available if archaeologists luckily turn up new Sothic notations definite enough to be used for chronological purposes.

Some Theories of the Eisodus and Exodus

The Egyptian chronology has many uses, and none has been more thoroughly explored than its relationship to the Chosen People. The Eisodus (entrance) into Egypt and the Exodus therefrom are historical events that have inspired a body of historical theorizing.

Dates for the Eisodus and Exodus, as well as many other events, could be found in the King James version of the Bible. They, of course, had no scriptural authority. They were simply the calculations of a learned seventeenth century bishop of the Anglican Church in Ireland named James Ussher. His dates for certain important events were as follows:

Birth of Abraham	1996 B.C.
Genesis 14:1	1917 B.C.
Eisodus (Joseph)	1729 B.C.
Exodus	1491 B.C.
Fall of Jericho	1451 B.C.
Saul	1095–1056 B.C.
David	1056–1015 B.C.
Solomon	1015–975 B.C.

The division of the kingdom into Judah, ruled by the Davidic line under Rehoboam, and Israel, ruled by an engineer named Jeroboam, thus came about 975 B.C. Ussher's dates were, of course, based on biblical evidence. Dates from other sources, save for the Classics, were not yet available.

The dating system used in the Bible has challenged scholars at least as far back as St. Jerome. In the nineteenth century a new school of biblical scholars known as the "Higher Critics" appeared, who reexamined the Bible as an historical document in an effort to discover the "traditions" that had been brought together into its various books. They eagerly received the archaeological information being unearthed during this period and used it in their work, but their efforts often drew criticisms from more orthodox believers who accused them of drawing inferences from possibilities derived from probabilities. Religionists of all connections, as well as agnostics, have taken a lively interest in the chronology of the ancient Hebrews.

To have a starting point in that chronology, it is necessary to provide a date for Abraham. How can that be done? Genesis 14:1 mentions four rulers who were the contemporaries of that Jewish patriarch: Amraphel, king of Shinar; Arioch, king of Ellasar; Chedorlaomer, king of Elam; and Tidal, king of nations. Shinar is a biblical name for Babylonia; Elam for the country east of it; Ellasar is probably Larsa. When Hammurabi emerged from the Babylonian darkness in the late nineteenth century, many scholars identified him with Amraphel, which would have placed Abraham (it was then thought) in the twenty-first century B.C. After World War II, however, this identification was generally abandoned for lack of evidence.

A German scholar named Frans M. Theodor Böhl suggested in various articles between 1924 and 1946 that Amraphel was Amur-pi-el, a ruler of Qatna, that the Tidal king was a Hittite ruler named Tudhaliyas, and that Arioch was a prince of Mari. These identifications would move Abraham forward in time, perhaps into the eighteenth century B.C. No one could say for sure. An eminent British scholar, Harold H. Rowley in his *From Joseph to Joshua* (1950) updated Abraham even further—into the seventeenth century B.C.

A multitude of identifications were proposed for the kings of Genesis 14:1 only to fail because supporting proof was lacking. In 1961, one of America's most eminent ancient historians, William F. Albright, presented his matured views on this subject. He believed that Abraham was by profession a merchant who spent part of his early life along a donkey caravan route between Ur and Harran in northern Mesopotamia and later between Damascus and Egypt. He accepted an identification of Chedorlaomer with Kudur Mabug, an Elamite ruler of Larsa who was an historic personality and who lived some time between the mid-nineteenth century and the early eighteenth century B.C., depending upon which chronology one accepts for Babylon I. Abraham seems to have found a temporary resting place in that general time area. Some recent histories of the Hebrews, however, seem intentionally to avoid dating this towering figure at the dawn of their history.

The next landmarks in Hebrew chronology involve the dates for the Eisodus and the Exodus. How do we date them? Two passages in the Bible are usually selected to aid in this process: in most versions, Exodus 12:40 states that the Hebrews sojourned in Egypt for 430 years, and I Kings 6:1 notes that Solomon built his temple in the fourth year of his reign, 480 years after the Exodus. The first of these statements is less definite because the Septuagint and the Samaritan Pentateuch assign the 430 years to the whole period between Abraham's departure from Harran and the Exodus. Ussher dated the building of the temple at 1011 B.C. and added 480 years to it to date the Exodus (1491 B.C.), and he apparently accepted the revised date for Joseph's entry into Egypt (1729 B.C.).

The facts of the Joseph story show that he and his people existed on terms of close friendship with the rulers of Egypt, and, as the Egyptians were normally a strongly ethnocentric people, such a relationship would not normally be expected. Many historians, following a statement by Josephus, have come to relate the Eisodus with the entry of the Hyksos into Egypt and identify Joseph and his people with one element in the coalition of peoples who conquered much of Egypt in the eighteenth and seventeenth centuries B.C.

The only other theory which might explain the friendly relationship between the Hebrew and Egyptian leaders at the time of the Eisodus was advanced and defended by Rowley in his work of 1951. The eccentric, almost monotheistic Amenhotep IV (Akhenaten) was selected by Rowley as the friendly pharaoh. Joseph became his chief minister, and Jacob later followed him into Egypt as described in Genesis 46:5–7. The facts Rowley provided to buttress his theory are too complex to be summarized here, and it would probably not be worthwhile to attempt such a summary because Rowley's theory has not acquired much of a following.

Most scholars accepted the Hyksos theory of the Eisodus, then moved on to date the Exodus. Fritz Hommel in 1898 employed the biblical date—the fifteenth century B.C.—for the Exodus, and James W. Jack in 1925 made an elaborate defense of it. The famous Hatshepsut became the pharaoh's daughter who rescued the infant Moses, and the even more prominent Thothmes III became the oppressor of the Hebrews.

A number of facts appeared that seemed to prove that the

Hebrews left Egypt and settled in Palestine during the fifteenth century B.C. The Amarna correspondence mentioned the "Habiru" as a people living in Palestine in the fourteenth century, and this same name came to light in tablets recovered from Nuzu, Ras Shamra, and other places. Ras Shamra tablets from the fifteenth century mentioned "Asher" and "Zebulon," two of the traditional twelve tribes of Israel. All of this fits the pattern of the fifteenth-century Exodus. Support for the theory arose also from the Jericho excavations of John Garstang reported in 1930. One of its walls appeared to have been breached and broken, and Garstang dated this wall between 1400–1370 B.C. at the latest. The most distinguished of all the early archaeologists, Flinders Petrie, visited the site and gave his general support to Garstang's interpretation.

Despite all of this evidence for a fifteenth-century Exodus, many scholars gradually abandoned the theory in favor of the thirteenth century. Their conversion seems to have arisen largely from two factors. First, even though the Egyptians were active in Palestine during the fifteenth to thirteenth centuries, the first explicit mention of Hebrews there is found on the Israel Stele (ca. 1220 B.C.): "Israel is desolated, and has no more seed." Had the Hebrews entered the area in the fifteenth century, scholars argued, it is likely that the Egyptians would have taken note of them.

A second objection has arisen from the archaeological discoveries in Palestine and the Trans-Jordan region. The excavations at Lachish, Bethel, and other places have provided archaeological evidence for a thirteenth century (or later) conquest. Nelson Glueck in 1940 declared that there were no settled populations in Trans-Jordan before the thirteenth century; hence, any Hebrews who came out of Egypt in the fifteenth century could not have encountered the states of Edom and Moab. They were not then in existence. The Jericho obstacle to the thirteenth-century Exodus theory was seemingly removed when another competent archaeological expedition of 1952–1958 announced that Garstang and Petrie had been wrong. The walls of Joshua's time had completely eroded away!

So the thirteenth century Exodus theory acquired an increasing number of scholarly adherents after World War II. If this theory is accurate, then Rameses II (or, much less probably, Merenptah) was the pharaoh of the Oppression, and the cities of Pithom and Raamses in the Delta region were the sites where the Hebrews labored. There is evidence to link Rameses II with these two cities.

But there still remained the "Habiru" difficulty. Obviously, the Hebrews could not have been both in Egypt and Syria-Palestine at the same time—or could they? Yes, they could, if some of the ingenious theories of scholars are accepted. Lewis B. Paton suggested in 1913 that only the Rachel tribes went into Egypt; the Habiru were the Leah tribes, and they had remained in Palestine. Samuel A. Mercer presented an even more elaborate explanation in 1922–1923—there were two Exoduses! Simeon and Asher came out first, then Judah, led by Moses, left Egypt during the reign of Merenptah. Olaf A. Toffteen in 1909 presented an even more involved theory: there had been both a double Eisodus and a double Exodus, the first taking place in 1877–1447 B.C. and the second in 1340–1144 B.C. Bernard D. Eerdmans (1947) distinguished between the Israelites and the Hebrews, and so on.

Most of these theories were designed to accommodate the "Habiru" in one way or another. Then the question arose, Did they need accommodation? How could one be sure the Habiru were the Hebrews? Moshe Greenberg in *The Hab/piru* (1955) concluded that this identification was open to a number of objections, none absolutely decisive, yet they were sufficiently strong to render the equation improbable. William F. Albright also firmly rejected the identification. So it seemed that the Habiru, like the walls of Jericho, needed no accommodation!

Whether one chooses to date the Exodus in the fifteenth or in the thirteenth century, the next phase in Israelite history (at this point, such a name is preferred) involves the Judges who ruled the tribes prior to the establishment of the kingdom of Saul. There were twelve Major Judges as well as many Minor Judges known only by name to be fitted into the chronology at this point. Those who hold to the fifteenth-century Exodus believe that their administrations were successive; defenders of the thirteenth century Exodus must necessarily overlap their careers. One thing is certain at this point—the geographical locus of Israelite history was now changed, and the chronology must be linked to that of Assyria rather than to the history of Egypt.

Babylon I: When It Flourished

A new era in the history of Tigris-Euphrates chronology might be said to have opened in 1937 when Thureau-Dangin, on the basis of credible evidence discovered at Mari, proved that the much-travelled Hammurabi was a younger contemporary of Shamshi-Adad I, the founder of the earliest of the Assyrian empires. Because the Assyrian ruler was known to have lived much later than the period generally assigned to Hammurabi, a reappraisal of the chronology was in order.

In 1940, Sidney Smith, a British scholar who had long been critical of the early dating of Hammurabi, published his monumental *Alalakh and Chronology*. An independent ruler in Alalakh named Yarim Lim, was the contemporary of both Hammurabi and the Khabur Ware style of pottery, which resembled that found in Egypt during the Hyksos Period. As Khabur ware could be traced to the 1800–1600 B.C. period, Hammurabi must have lived during that time frame. Smith then turned to the Venus Tablets and found that a cycle had begun in the 1640s. He assigned 1646 B.C. to Ammi-zaduga; this meant Hammurabi was fixed in the 1792–1750 B.C. period. Babylon I as a whole flourished between 1894–1595 B.C. In the latter year the town was sacked by the Hittites, and the Kassite Dynasty was established as the new rulers of Babylonia.

The Smith chronology attracted a considerable number of scholarly adherents. Then, in 1942, Arno Poebel published his translation of the Assyrian king list from Khorsabad, which had been discovered in 1932 by a University of Chicago expedition, and the whole subject was reopened. This list was in better condition and more nearly complete than were the earlier Nassouhi and Ashur B Lists. The Assyrians had invented a clever mnemonics device associated with the priestly office of "limmu." This office was bestowed yearly upon a different official, who was the eponym, that is, the year was named for the holder. A few of these limmu lists had been discovered, and it was assumed that the scribes who had drawn up the Khorsabad list had such lists that went back to the thirty-third ruler in Assyrian history. If so, they would have had a precise recorded chronology through most of the centuries. Poebel simply added up the reigns of the Assyrian rulers from Tiglathpileser III, who began to rule in 744 B.C., and Shamsi Adad I, and this provided a 1726 B.C. date for the latter ruler. As he was an elder contemporary of Hammurabi, the latter could not have lived during 1792–1750 B.C. as Smith believed. So another revision was inevitable.

At this point (1942) the eminent American scholar, William F. Albright, entered the controversy. He believed that the Egyptians had a fairly substantial empire in Syria during the Middle Kingdom and that Hammurabi could not have created his own empire in that region until Egyptian authority had been disestablished some time late in the eighteenth century. On the other hand, the date provided by Poebel for Shamsi-Adad I—1726 B.C.—assigned zero years to the reigns of Ashur-rabi I and Ashur-nadin-ahhe I, who lived in the fifteenth century B.C., and whose reign lengths had been broken away from the tablet. Albright gave them twenty-two years, which pushed Shamshi-Adad I back to 1748 B.C. Another Venus cycle, this one in the sixteenth century, was discovered, and it became the basis for Albright's 1728–1686 B.C. date for Hammurabi. Interestingly enough, a German historian named Friedrich Cornelius, using other evidence, arrived at almost the same dates that very year, and this became known as the Albright-Cornelius chronology.

The reader cannot possibly appreciate the scholarly debate that followed unless he understands the reason for the historian's longing to establish exact dates. What do a few years matter, one might ask? They matter because a single year is a long time, and it may be filled with events of decisive political importance. Looking back over the centuries of ancient history, one can easily forget this fact, and, if one does, one will find oneself lost within a maze of disjointed, unrelated events—historyless and, therefore, meaningless. Scholars longed to nail down the Babylon I Dynasty securely in time. If they could do so, they could begin with confidence to assemble around it the facts they knew about other political entities. They had the Assyrian king list, an indefinite Hittite king list, a partial list of the Mitannian rulers, a number of later Babylonian lists, as well as the prominent figures in the history of the Hebrews—all of these might fall into their proper places in history if only the Babylonian pattern could be firmly established.

Two years after Albright presented his chronology, another eminent scholar, Arthur Ungnad, published his views, which were close to those of Smith. But David Sidersky and Francois Thureau-Dangin felt that both Smith and Albright had been too enthusiastic in their updating, and sought an earlier date for Babylon I. Then, Michael B. Rowton in 1948 came out in favor of Albright, and Bartel L. van den Waerden demonstrated the mathematical probability that the Albright-Cornelius chronology was more accurate than that of Smith.

In 1951, a German authority on the Hittites, Albrecht Goetze, launched a major attack on the later chronologies. The Hittite ruler, Mursilis I, was known to have sacked Babylon and to have ended the Babylon I dynasty. Sidersky and Thureau-Dangin believed this took place in 1651 B.C., while Smith placed it in 1595 B.C., Cornelius in 1531 B.C., and

Schubert in 1500 B.C. The next established date in Hittite history involved Tudhaliyas I, who lived about 1450 B.C. Between Mursilis I and Tudhaliyas I there had been nine Hittite rulers who represented seven generations. It seemed impossible to crowd them into the 1531–1450 B.C. period, or even the 1595–1450 B.C. period, so Goetze ranged himself on the side of Sidersky and Thureau-Dangin.

The following year, Rowton broke a lance in favor of Albright. He pointed out that the period of Hittite history between Mursilis and Tudhaliyas was a troubled one during which many rulers were murdered and showed that a similar period in Babylonian history featured kings with very short reigns. Albright also answered Goetze. He insisted that Egyptian influence in Syria-Palestine remained strong until 1730 B.C., so it would have been impossible for Hammurabi to create his empire until late in the eighteenth century. Goetze, however, was unconvinced. Egyptian influence in Syria had ended long before 1730 B.C., he declared, and reiterated his objections to the short chronologies based on his theory of the seven Hittite generations. Albright, in turn, replied to Goetze denying the seven generations which seemed to form the substance of his opponent's argument.

The whole situation was surveyed again in 1954 by Benno Landsberger in his "Assyriche Königliste und 'Dunkles Zeitalter.' " As in the case of the others, it is impossible to do justice here to his arguments, which were based on a wide range of historical evidence. Some of his more telling points, however, were derived from Babylonian sources, the King List A, the Agumkagrime Chronicle, and the Synchronous History; his objections were also based on the alleged crowding of the rulers in the shorter chronologies. One of his most telling arguments involved Gandish, whom all of the Babylonian sources made the first Kassite ruler in Babylon, yet both Smith and Albright, in order to achieve a certain synchronization with the Assyrian king list, had ignored him in favor of a ruler named Agum II. In his conclusion, Landsberger condemned the Albright chronology as too short, admitted the possibility of the Smith chronology, and expressed his own preference for an 1829 B.C. date for Hammurabi.

Goetze, his position much strengthened by the Landsberger analysis, continued his debate with Albright during 1956–1957. Then came a serious defection from the Albright camp. Michael B. Rowton in 1958 produced a detailed study of the evidence. He pointed out that the Alalakh pottery could be used to confirm all three chronologies, the High (Sidersky), the Middle (Smith), and the Low (Albright). The Assyrian king list, however, favored the Middle and the Low, and Babylonian evidence supported the Middle one. The High chronology could not be squared with either the Venus cycle or recent radiocarbon dates, so it was rejected. Finally, as it was difficult to reconcile the Low chronology with the Kassite Dynasty in Babylon, Rowton abandoned Albright and gave his support to Smith.

By this time Albright was beleaguered but unbowed. The American scholar continued to respond to his critics, countering every objection and point raised by them effectively and dispassionately. His last article on the subject in 1965 noted that 1728 B.C. might not have been Hammurabi's first year, but it was the one in harmony with the Venus cycle. "Professor Goetze is always an honest debater," he once wrote, "and he always brings new data to bear on disputed questions, whatever one's reactions to his interpretations may be." Certainly the same must be said of the gallant Albright.

This long debate brought into sharper focus the relative values of the various king lists. The Hittite list suffered in 1953 when it was discovered there were two rulers named "Suppululiumas" whose ancestors had similar names. In his study of 1975, Johannes Lehmann observed no one could be sure which of them had which ancestors in what order. A solar eclipse in the year 10 of Mursilis II lost its value when scholars failed to agree regarding its date. Such uncertainty obtained that Friedrich Cornelius in his *Geschichte der*

Hethiter (1973) declared that the last three rulers named by
Goetze in his 1951 article probably did not have an historical
existence, which tended to weaken the seven-generations
argument.

Nor did the Babylonian sources come out of the fray un-
scathed. In an article of 1958, Hayim Tadmor demonstrated
that, between Burnaburiash in the fourteenth century B.C. and
Nabu-shum-libur in the eleventh century, there were four
different dates possible for each of the rulers. Landsberger's
objection regarding the misplacing of Gandish, however, remained. Gandish should—and could—be put in his proper
place.

Even the prestigious Assyrian king list suffered. As Rowton
pointed out in 1958, some of the dates of the list could not be
reconciled with the chronological statements made by the
Assyrian monarchs. Further, the list involved the problem of
the "tupisu" rulers. Poebel took the word "DUB-pi-su" to
mean zero years, that is, such kings reigned within the remaining months of the previous monarch before the beginning
of the next regnal year. This involved the two rulers whose
reign lengths were missing and five others whom Poebel dated
1648 B.C. Some other scholars translated "tupisu" to mean
"for awhile," which would, of course, destroy the value of the
list for the purposes of exact dating. Finally, in 1954, I. G.
Gelb showed there were minor variations in the reign lengths
of certain Assyrian rulers in the different versions of the list.
Despite these defects, the Khorsabad list still is a cornerstone
of Near Eastern chronology, especially from the mid-second
millennium down to the fall of Assyria.

Israeli Kings and Assyrian Monarchs

While the scholarly world did not reach a firm decision as
to whether Smith or Albright was correct in dating Babylon
I, there has been for many decades a consensus on the subject
of the first millennium B.C. Assyrian limmu lists have long
been available for the years 892–662 B.C., and a fixed point

within the lists was discovered quite early. This was an eclipse in year 10 of Ashurdan III's reign which has been dated 15 June 763 B.C. This chronology appears to be as certain as one can expect in this area of history.

What has made the Assyrian lists of this era so interesting to scholars is that certain datable contacts were made between the Assyrians and the Israelites, and they are thus synchronized with biblical chronology. Two of the most important occurred during the reign of Shalmaneser III, who fought King Ahab of Israel at the battle of Karkar in 853 B.C. (or, in earlier accounts, 854 B.C.), and collected tribute from King Jehu of Israel in 841 B.C.

The discovery of these contacts was made shortly after the tablets from Ashurbanipal's library arrived in Britain. First it caused a sensation; then gave rise to consternation. If the chronologies provided by the Bible were followed, these points of contact seemingly could not be made. If the synchronizations were made, the reign lengths would not fit the chronology of the Bible. How could this be? Jules Oppert in 1868 postulated a break in the limmu list. George Smith, who had translated the documents, decided that the Ahab and Jehu of the Assyrian inscriptions were not those mentioned in the Bible. He also pointed out certain gross errors in the Assyrian documents as well as conflicts of fact in their accounts of the battle of Karkar, his chronology ignored the synchronizations, dated Saul at 981 B.C., and continued down to the destruction of Jerusalem in 587 B.C.

Sir Henry Rawlinson and a German scholar named Eberhard Schrader were less convinced of the biblical dates. They proposed an important identification. II Kings 19 notes: "And Pul the king of Assyria came against the land; and Menahem gave Pul a thousand talents of silver." I Chronicles 5:26 explains: "And the God of Israel stirred up the spirit of Pul king of Assyria, and the spirit of Tiglath-pileser king of Assyria, and he carried them away." Pul, they said, was Tiglathpileser III, and this permitted them to shorten the chronology. From

Classical sources they could also find a date for Solomon. Josephus noted that Carthage had been founded 155 years and 8 months after the accession of Hiram of Tyre, a contemporary of Solomon, and Roman writers dated Carthage 815 (814) B.C. Thus, Hiram came to the throne about 971 B.C. Sheshonk I of Egypt, who ruled toward the end of Solomon's reign, became Pharaoh in 935 B.C. These two dates permitted Rawlinson and Schrader to place Solomon's forty-year reign between 970–930 B.C. Many scholars, however, rejected this identification of Pul even though this meant the Bible had added an unknown Assyrian ruler and was therefore inaccurate.

The mystery of Pul was cleared up by Eduard Meyer in his *Geschichte des Altertums* (1926). Tiglathpileser had also ruled Babylon, and a Babylonian source noted that his throne name there was "Pulu." The key to the confusing passage in Chronicles was the singular pronoun employed. If the "and" is changed to "even," a different sense shines through; this was a stride forward, but the chronology still remained controversial, and various scholars divided the Hebrew Kingdom anywhere from 929 to 921 B.C.

William F. Albright published "The Chronology of the Divided Monarchy of Israel" in 1945, and his system still has adherents today. Like Smith, he accepted the classical date of 814 B.C. for the founding of Carthage, which was year 7 of a Tyrean ruler named Pygmalion. By comparing the chronologies of Tyre and the Israelite Kingdom, he concluded that Solomon began his temple in 959 B.C., the year 4 of his reign; that wise ruler therefore must have died about 923–922 B.C. Confirmation came from a statement by Josephus that the temple was begun 145 years before the founding of Carthage.

By the time Albright wrote, the chronologies of Judah and Israel had perplexed and confounded biblical scholars for some eighty-five years. Albright concluded, perhaps wearily, that the dates in the Scriptures must have been corrupted through copying and recopying over hundreds of years, and he therefore felt free in his chronologies to reject about fourteen of them. So, in the end, his solution was no solution at all. The chronologies of the Bible were synchronized with those of Assyria without much regard for the biblical dates.

One biblical scholar was not yet ready to give up. Edwin R. Thiele, with some help from William A. Irwin and such lights as George C. Cameron and Richard A. Parker, published *The Mysterious Numbers of the Hebrew Kings* in 1951. Thiele assumed that the biblical dates were accurate but that the chronological practices of the Jewish scribes, like those of many other ancient peoples, were complex.

Some ancient rulers numbered their regnal years from the moment of their accession to the throne (the non-accession-year system); others began their year I with the next new year's day after they attained power (the accession-year system). It was well known that the ancient Hebrews had two calendar years, one that began with the month of Nisan in the spring, the other with Tishri in the fall. Some evidence was at hand to show that Judah began her year with Tishri and Israel chose Nisan instead. Furthermore, during most of the period of the divided kingdom, Judah (the legitimate succession-state of David) used the accession-year system, while Israelite rulers numbered their years from the time they actually came to the throne. The situation was complicated further by the assumption that scribes of Judah would use their system when recounting reigns in both kingdoms and those of Israel would use the other system.

With this in mind and beginning with 853 B.C. when Ahab of Israel died, Thiele counted back the years of the Israelite kings to Jeroboam, a total of seventy-eight, and came up with 931 B.C. for the division of the kingdom after Solomon's death. In Judah, where David had set a precedent by establishing a co-regency with Solomon before his death, the system of co-regencies seems to have been common; Asa, Jehoshaphat, Jehoram, Amaziah, Azariah, Jotham, Ahaz, Hezekiah, and Manasseh all were assumed by Thiele to have had father-son co-regencies for various periods of time. In Israel this was not customary. Only Jehoash and Jeroboam II were believed to have had a co-regency, but the reigns of Omri and Pekah were thought to have overlapped with those of other rulers. Under the Thiele system, the chronologies of Judah and Israel found in the Bible generally agree with each other and can be synchronized with the contact points of Assyrian history.

One difficulty that remained for some time was the name of the ruler who destroyed Samaria, the capital of Israel. In II Kings 17:3-6 and 18:9-10 the Assyrian king involved seems to be Shalmaneser V, known to have died in 722 B.C. But when the annals of his successor, Sargon II, were discovered and translated, it was found that Sargon claimed to have taken Samaria at the beginning of his reign. His claim was given credence until the Babylonian chronicle substantiated Shalmaneser's right to this dubious honor. Siegfried Herrmann in his recent history of Israel (1973) notes that scholars today (in Germany at least) generally reject the statement of Sargon.

The work of Thiele provides a strong structure for the histories of Judah and Israel, and the histories of the two nations can be synchronized with those of Assyria, Damascus, Tyre, and Egypt in a convincing manner. But certain imperfections remain. Several synchronisms, especially those found in II Kings 17:1, and 18:1, 9-10 simply cannot be accommodated within it. Then there is the date for the death of Josiah in the spring of 609 B.C., one year before the date established by Thiele's system. Thiele discussed this difficulty in an article of 1956.

Since Thiele published his work, other scholars, particularly in Germany, have presented other chronologies, but the results have not been impressive. At the present time, the choice seems to be between the Albright system, which tends to ignore the biblical dating, and that of Thiele, which goes a long way toward substantiating it. In Kings, one finds tantalizing references to what seems to have been more detailed Israelite historical documents that have been lost. Perhaps when the deep foundations of some new building in Jerusalem are laid, the workers will come upon these ancient records. What a sensation that would cause!

Before closing this interesting topic, some note should be taken of what might be called the Swedish school of biblical chronology that has been active in recent years. Knut Stenring published *The Enclosed Garden* in 1966, and his work has since been analyzed by mathematician Gerhard Larsson in *The Secret System,* published in 1973. This is probably the most exhaustive study of biblical chronology up to this time, for Stenring's tables begin with the year of Creation and date most of the biblical events from that event, according to the chronology in the Scriptures, down to the fall of Judah— using three different calendars! The Exodus, for example, occurred on 18 September, 2,445 years after Creation according to the lunar calendar; 15 January, 2,372 years after Creation by the solar calendar; and 3 June, 2,370 years after Creation by the standard calendar; or 1466 B.C. according to our time reckoning. Larsson describes in some detail the uses of this interesting system.

During the sixteen decades since Caviglia began poking around the Great Pyramid of Khufu in 1817, our knowledge of the ancient world has expanded enormously. At that time, history before the Greeks was shrouded in mystery. Peoples such as the Minoans, Hittites, Sumerians, and Mitannians were wholly unknown or were mere names unencumbered by historical attachments. Even today, the periphery of the ancient Near East holds countless mysteries, and the heartlands —the Tigris-Euphrates valley, Syria-Palestine, Egypt, and eastern Asia Minor—still contain vexing historical problems, especially before 1500 B.C.

Still, a towering historical structure has emerged, and the question might be posed, How long are the expensive and exhausting efforts likely to continue? The splendid project of

Europe and its derivatives to recover the history of the world was originally stimulated by religious and intellectual considerations, both of which are operative today, and there is little reason to doubt that important finds will continue to be made if the spades of the archaeologists continue to dig. It seems that man, as soon as he invented the written word, had a vision of that precarious form of immortality that comes with finding a niche in the collective memory of mankind and recorded his deeds as best he could in the hope that future generations would care to read of them. We can thus be sure that tomorrow, if not today, some field worker will casually turn up another tablet or slab that will fill another open space in the vast jigsaw puzzle. But we must remember that the reconstruction project is unique, that contemporary concerns easily overslaugh those of the past, and that the future of ancient history will depend upon the persistence of objective scholarship in a changing and chaotic world.

7

Progress in
Remote Periods

HERETOFORE WE HAVE BEEN concerned primarily with the
reconstruction of the history of the great Near Eastern states
during the three millennia preceding the Christian Era. This
endeavor, however, represents merely a fraction of the time
span in which archaeologists and their allies undertake their
investigations. Much of their scholarly effort is directed toward
centuries even more remote and dealing with the preliterate
cultures that arose in many parts of the globe. For our purposes
it will be sufficient to discuss briefly some of the facts uncovered about the preliterate cultures of the ancient Near
East and to see how they were organized. In this geographical
area changes of interpretation of considerable importance
have taken place since World War II.

If we think of the history of mankind as a book, the first
three chapters would be headed "Palaeolithic," "Mesolithic,"
and "Neolithic." Written history begins in some plans at this
point, but where it does not do so, the next three chapters
may be headed the "Chalcolithic Age," "Bronze Age," and
"Iron Age." A system of dividing early history into periods
named for materials used for tools and weapons was first ad-

vanced by a Dane, Christian Thomsen, who wrote of the Stone, Bronze, and Iron ages of man in the mid-nineteenth century. The system is a convenient means of bringing some sort of order into a maze of archaeological complexities.

While the Palaeolithic Age lasted much longer than all of the others combined, the giant step forward into what we call civilized life was taken at the outset of the Neolithic Age, a change so important that V. Gordon Childe coined the term "Neolithic Revolution" to describe it. At this point man settled down to an agricultural existence, and a more complex social structure began to evolve. Neolithic culture used to be associated with both farming and pottery-making until it became evident that most of the earlier Neolithic cultures did not manufacture fired pottery. Fired pottery, and the smelting of copper seem to have evolved in tandem, and this development takes us into the Chalcolithic Age. Later, when tin was added to copper, the Bronze Age began.

For the first century, more or less, of archaeological development, depending on how one chooses to date the study, the remains of all three prehistoric periods were uncovered in abundance, and the problem of attaching dates to them was acute and perplexing. Pottery sequences could be established in some places, and the contemporaneousness of a level at one site with a certain level at another could be established, but the scholarly guesses as to absolute dating varied widely. At sites where no pottery was present, the dating problem was insoluble. Fortunately, in recent years various branches of science have offered a helping hand to archaeologists.

In the most remote periods, new means of dating minerals are of some value. The disintegration of single radioactive substance, such as thorium or uranium, takes place at a fixed rate, and the age of a rock specimen containing such an element is estimated on the basis of the progress of this disintegration at any given time. Other methods of dating minerals are based on the disintegration of potassium argon and by bombarding a specimen with alpha particles. The accuracy of all of these methods is in inverse relationship to the age of the specimen involved.

Ingenious methods have been discovered to cast new light on the most recent Ice Age, the last half million or so years of the earth's history. Glaciers melted on four different occasions, and in so doing laid down annual deposits consisting of soft sand at the bottom and darker clay at the top, which together are termed a "varve." Where available the varves are as accurate a means of counting years as tree rings, which are sometimes also employed in chronology. A second method involves pollen, which survives almost indefinitely. By analyzing pollen in a site it is possible to reconstruct the flora of the period, which, in turn, provides clues to weather conditions of the time.

Of more importance to those working in later periods of prehistory are the fluorine method and the petroanalysis technique. When bones lie in the earth, they absorb fluorine; this produces an insoluble compound called fluorapatite. Rapid at first, this process slows down until a saturation point is reached in 500,000 years. The age of a specimen is calculated on the basis of how far it is from the saturation point. Unfortunately for scientists the process is speeded up or inhibited by environmental factors. Petroanalysis, which attempts to trace the materials used in pottery to their place of origin, is still in an early state of development.

A scientific dating method called C-14 attracted widespread attention in 1949 when it was described by an American chemist, Willard F. Libby. Both plant and animal life take in radioactive carbon during their lifetimes until the intake is balanced by the distintegration. When the plant or animal dies, only the disintegration continues (in a manner reminiscent of the story of the man who walked half the distance to town the first day, half of the remaining distance the second, and so on, and, of course, never quite got there). Libby calculated that half of the radioactivity would disappear after 5,568 years. While this figure has been modified, the method of measuring the age of the specimen by the lessening of its radioactivity remains the same. The rate of disintegration is believed to be wholly divorced from environmental factors.

Unfortunately, the technique was publicized widely and too much was expected of it. In 1959 Elizabeth K. Ralph reported that the dates established for three Egyptian rulers by the University of Pennsylvania using this method were all too recent. Doubts were momentarily quelled in 1963 when Libby himself used his method to date five rulers of Egypt with stunning success. As it turned out, others could not employ it nearly as effectively. The dates derived for Egyptian rulers published by the British Museum in 1966 and 1969 were consistently too low, and those obtained at the same institution in 1971 were startling. Five samples from the tomb of Intef gave up dates that ranged between 1550 and 630 B.C.

About this time Professor C. W. Ferguson of the University of Arizona discovered a means of "calibrating," that is, correcting, the C-14 dates. He collected specimens of the long-lived bristlecone pine tree, living and dead, whose ages could be accurately determined by counting the tree rings. These covered the centuries back to 5000 B.C. Specimens with known ages were tested in radiocarbon laboratories, and the C-14 dates were found to be too recent. Since then mathematical curves have been devised to correct the C-14 dates, none of them wholly satisfactory. But C-14 dates are now in widespread use.

Understanding just what a C-14 date means is not easy. In some studies the raw C-14 dates are followed by an "ad," or a "bc" (sometimes "bp," meaning "before the present"), whereas the calibrated dates will be followed by an "AD," "BC" or "BP". Dates usually also are followed by plus-minus deviations. Take, for example, the C-14 date 2500 B.C. plus-minus 150 years. This means the radiocarbon technicians who determined the date believe that 2500 B.C. is the most probable date of the specimen, but they are by no means certain.

There is a 66 percent probability the date lies within the 2700–2400 B.C. range, a 95 percent probability that it falls between 2850–2250 B.C., and almost a certainty that it lies between 3000–2100 B.C.

The C-14 method is still under study, and I have been assured recently by a laboratory that space-age techniques are being called upon to take the kinks out of the calibration curves and to reduce the standard deviations. At the moment the method is of little value to historians, but for archaeologists C-14 and the other aids have created welcome footholds on the slippery slopes of the distant past.

Archaeologists, both before and after World War II, have been so successful in uncovering and examining prehistoric sites in the Near East that it would be impossible to adequately describe here the recovery of the preliterate cultures in any depth. The geographical areas of interest have traditionally included Egypt, the Tigris-Euphrates Valley area, Syria-Palestine, and Anatolia, and, farther to the west, Crete and Mycenaean Greece. Here we must limit ourselves to six brief discussions of the development of outlines of prehistory in certain important areas and some of the continuing problems still to be solved by archaeologists and historians.

The land of the pharaohs, due partly to the chronology drawn up by Sir William Flinders Petrie, has long been regarded as extremely ancient. Petrie distinguished five prehistoric Egyptian cultures, named for various sites in Egypt, called the Tasian, Badarian, Amratian, Gerzean, and Semainean, the first of which he dated 9000 B.C. After World War II a Palaeolithic campsite, called the Sebekian culture, was dated 12,290 B.C. and 12,150 B.C. by the C-14 method, but the same method applied to Petrie cultures revealed that they were much later than Petrie thought them to be. In a study of 1964, another of the older archaeologists, William C. Hayes, provided a much shorter chronology based largely on C-14 dates. The onset of the Neolithic period of Egypt was no earlier than 5000 B.C., the Amratian culture advanced eighteen hundred years to 3783 B.C. and the Gerzean about fourteen hundred years to 3616 B.C.

The fact is that Egypt was hardly suited to stage the Neolithic Revolution. None of the important cereals or domestic animals were native to that country. Both had to be imported from areas where settled agriculture had already arisen. Egyptologists nevertheless could still boast that the chronology of Egypt continues to hold the center court in historic times and that the chronologies of many other ancient states depend upon it for their place in time.

Turning now to the Tigris-Euphrates Valley, it should be noted immediately that sharp differences of opinion have always obtained regarding the identity of the people who gave birth to the splendid third millennium B.C. culture there. That they were migrants is attested by the absence of Palaeolithic sites in the valley, and the earliest cultures had some knowledge of metal work. Before World War II, scholars in this area were deeply concerned with the interrelationships of the Ubaid, Uruk, and Jemdet Nasr cultures, all found in the valley. Archaeologists in those days tended to trace major changes in pottery styles to intruders, and these cultures were therefore attached to one or another of the peoples known to have been in the valley in early times, namely, the Sumerians, the Akkadians, and the Elamites. Their identities were sharply distinguished by their languages. At the time it was fascinating to follow the controversy, as the various authorities marshaled the meager evidence available to them to support their points of view. They never reached an agreement, however, and historians were left to draw their own conclusions in the matter of precedence. With the discovery in 1948 of another culture, called Eridu, another dimension has been added to the continuing controversy.

But it is probably accurate to state that, after World War II, the major focus of interest has migrated northward. Scholars were not so much concerned with who started the valley civilization as where the Neolithic culture first appeared in the general area. It was logical to assume that Neolithic culture began in a place where rain agriculture was possible rather than in one which had to depend on a sophisticated irrigation system for water.

During the decade after World War II several Neolithic cultures came to light north of the valley. Robert J. and Linda Braidwood, who were active in this recovery, discussed the new situation in an article of 1952, a time when the C-14 dates were not reliable. Three cultures were present, called Hassuna, Matarrah, and Jarmo. As Hassuna pottery sherds had been found on the surface of mounds in the Jarmo region, it was clear that the latter was older than the former, and, as the Matarrah pottery seemed like an impoverished version of Hassuna, it was assumed they were close together in time. The Braidwoods concluded that Jarmo was the oldest of the three and the other two were contemporary for a major portion of their duration.

When the C-14 method was applied, the Jarmo culture turned out to be about two thousand years older than Braidwood had guessed in 1952. Today it is generally dated about 6750 B.C., and the others are regarded as about a thousand years younger. The Braidwoods had noted that the Jarmo culture seemed dynamic, due possibly to the fact that its people had created a new way of life. The Jarmo people lived in mud huts, cultivated barley and two types of wheat, and had domesticated sheep, goats, and pigs. They still used stone tools, many of them called microliths.

In the postwar years other sites have been uncovered north of the valley which attest to the evolution of civilization through the Upper Palaeolithic, Mesolithic, and Neolithic stages. Prehistory there is given an opening date of 35,000 B.C. Since all these discoveries, important and complex questions have arisen regarding their interrelationships and the relationships they bear to the origins of the valley civilization. Whatever may be the conclusions reached, one fact is clear enough—in the area north of the valley man ceased his wanderings and settled down at a very early date. Whether or not it was the earliest is still far from clear.

The Palestine area, due chiefly to its religious importance, has attracted archaeologists and their allies for more than a century. Since 1925 it has taken on historical importance for a purely secular reason—the finds there have strengthened its claims to being a cradle of human civilization. Summarizing the progress of Palestinian archaeology between the two wars, Chester C. McCown in *The Ladder of Progress in Palestine* (1943) wrote enthusiastically: "The prehistorian is 100,000 years nearer the Palestinian Adam than he was when the war ended. From 6000 B.C. to 75,000 or 100,000, not to mention 500,000 years ago, is a tremendous leap."

This new era in Palestinian archaeology opened in 1925 when an Englishman, F. Turville-Petre, discovered the first stratified deposits in Palestine in two caves near the Sea of Galilee, one of which gave up the skull of a Neanderthal man, long known in Europe as a not-quite-human species. Thereafter the major figure in Palestinian archaeology was Dorothy Garrod, whose all-female expeditions made such important discoveries that their leader was awarded a professorship at Cambridge University, the first woman to be so honored.

Garrod's first, and highly significant, discovery came in 1928 when she was digging in a cave ten miles northwest of Jerusalem. She uncovered what she called the "Natufian culture," named for Wad' en-Natuf, the place of discovery. This was a splendid start. The autumn of the same year some workmen blasting rock in the Mt. Carmel Range to build a breakwater near Haifa came across some flint tools. Garrod promptly went there and worked until 1934.

Three caves were involved. Digging in the first of these, Garrod learned that the Natufian culture went through two stages, and the flint sickles she discovered indicated that the Natufians reaped—whether they sowed was another matter. Abundant skeletal remains identified the Natufians with the

Mediterranean race, one widely dispersed through the Middle East and Europe in ancient times. Even more important, perhaps, were the layers below the Natufian, which it was thought pushed the archaeological history of Palestine some 75,000 years into the past. Her findings in another cave confirmed and supplemented the information she derived from the first one.

After some preliminary testings in a third cave, Garrod turned the project over to Theodore D. McCown of the University of California. He subsequently uncovered another partial skeleton of the Neanderthal type, which was packed off to a distinguished physical anthropologist in London for examination. Interest in so-called fossil men in those days was much more intense than it is now, and this "Mt. Carmel," or "Palestine," man caused much discussion, as he seemed more nearly human than the Neanderthalers. Despite certain advanced characteristics, he has yet to be admitted to the species *sapiens.*

While Garrod was making her name in the caves of Palestine, John Garstang of the University of Liverpool chose to rework Jericho, where a German team had labored during 1907–1909. The Germans concluded that the Israelites had taken the city about 1600 B.C., and part of his mission was to reexamine the evidence. This was not easy, for the Germans had left heaps of debris on the site. Garstang worked many years (1929–1934) and finally concluded the Israelites had destroyed the city between 1385 and 1250 B.C. Much more important in the long run was his discovery of a Mesolithic stratum at Jericho whose artifacts resembled those of Garrod's Natufian culture.

The antiquity of Palestine was thus well attested prior to World War II. Since that time, archaeologists, using the advanced techniques at their disposal, have created a fairly sharp picture of the remote history of Palestine. During the late Palaeolithic era, Palestine was blessed with large lakes, and the climate was salubrious. Palestine man, now dated

35,000 B.C., thus lived and moved in a most favorable environment. But the climate changed later in that period. The land dried out, and living conditions became more severe. Under these circumstances, the Natufians, who had arrived on the scene by 10,000 B.C., took to the caves, but they were otherwise a fairly advanced people. They seem to have hovered in a lengthy twilight zone between a pastoral and an agricultural economy. Imaginative observers believe that men first domesticated animals, but it was women who planted the first seeds. Even after the techniques of primitive agriculture were known, some of the early peoples seem to have clung to their long-established habit of wandering.

Kathleen Kenyon went to Jericho during 1952–1958, and her discoveries there were significant, even exciting. She laid to rest (or so it seems) the walls controversy by concluding that the Bronze Age town of Joshua's time has practically eroded away. But while laying one controversy to rest, she helped to create another. Her excavations proved the existence of a pre-pottery Neolithic culture at Jericho and furthermore that it was a fortified city at a very early date.

Emmanuel Anati in 1962 summarized the problem that the antiquity of Jericho had created. Jarmo, merely a farming village, had flourished in the seventh millennium B.C.; Hacilar, also a farming community, had been dated 5590 B.C., and in Egypt there was no village life until the late fifth millennium B.C. Yet there stood Jericho, which knew only incipient farming, but was a fully developed town with a wall dating to 6850 B.C. by the C-14 method! He concluded that this "first city" came into being through trade in salt, sulphur, and bitumen probably with Anatolia and settlements on the shores of the Mediterranean. William F. Albright accepted the fact of Jericho's venerable origins and suggested that similar towns might have been scattered over the Middle East during the 7000–5000 B.C. period, but some archaeologists did not and simply rejected the C-14 date for the city. The advocates of an ancient Jericho, however, did not retreat. Avraham Negev in his *Archaeology in the Land of the Bible* (1976) traced the fortified city back to the eighth millennium B.C.!

If the findings in Palestine have been exciting and controversial, the same might be said of those in present-day Turkey. Before World War II, the prehistory of this region, save for Troy in the far northwest, was almost as blank as that of Palestine before 1925. Bedrich Hrozny, whom we have mentioned earlier, uncovered an Assyrian colony at Kültepe in 1925, which established an early connection between Anatolia and the Mesopotamian region, and H. H. von der Osten drew up a chronology for Anatolia in 1933 that dated the Neolithic period about 3500 B.C. In those days, perhaps understandably, scholarly interest was focused on later periods of the area's history, especially the time of the Hittites.

Since World War II a number of Palaeolithic sites have been located and excavated in Anatolia, enough to establish that it went through the Lower, Middle, and Upper Palaeolithic stages of development. Mesolithic sites have been lacking, and it was those of the Neolithic Era that attracted the most attention.

In 1961 a British archaeologist, James Mellaart, began to dig at Catal Hüyük, and the investigation of this thirty-two acre site, the largest Neolithic settlement in the entire Middle East, still continues. Many interesting features, including some "firsts" in prehistory, have been uncovered. The Catal Hüyük people lived in mud-brick houses, had a religion featuring a mother goddess and bulls, created the earliest wall paintings known to history, manufactured the oldest known textiles, created pottery and copper and lead ornaments, and used stone tools. They had a well-developed agriculture and had domesticated a limited number of animals. Their culture seemed well in advance of that at Jarmo, but the C-14 method dated the site 6800–5700 B.C., about the same time as the Mesopotamian site.

Space permits the mention of only a limited number of the important archaeological sites worked in Anatolia since World

War II. Listing them in probable chronological order, next came Mersin in the far southeastern corner, excavated in 1946–47, a Neolithic settlement that is dated 6000–3500 B.C. Its lower levels lie beneath the water table and are thus beyond the reach of excavators. Work began at Can Hasan, south of Catal Hüyük, in 1961, and it proved to be a Chalcolithic settlement featuring two-story houses dating to about 5000 B.C. Beycesultan first saw the light during 1954–1959 and is another Chalcolithic site with a continuous history extending between 4500–1200 B.C. Alaca Hüyük, whose gold and silver hoards have excited much scholarly speculation, is more recent and probably flourished during 3000–1200 B.C.

The discovery of these ancient settlements in Anatolia was exciting because Turkey is a sort of geographical bridge between the Near East and Europe. Did the people in this area create their cultures independently and live in isolation? Or did they derive their inspiration from even more advanced cultures elsewhere? Did their ideas diffuse into Syria in the southeast? Or southwest into Crete?

U Bahadir Alkim in *Anatolia I* (1968) stated flatly that Anatolian influence on Crete was no longer a probability but a certainty. Could it be that the splendid Minoan culture that has fascinated historians ever since Evans uncovered it early in the twentieth century was merely a reflection of an original culture in Anatolia?

When we come to this problem, we begin to tread on the sacred soil of Europe, and the progress of prehistory in Crete and Mycenaean Greece is a story in itself.

Strictly speaking neither Crete nor Mycenaean Greece can be classified among the preliterate cultures. As we have seen earlier, a kind of picture writing and the Linear A script were developed on the island of Crete, and the Greeks employed the Linear B script in Mycenaean times—at least the majority of scholars think so. But the first two have resisted decipherment, and the documents so far translated from Linear B have been singularly uninformative insofar as political history is concerned. It seems ironic that the Greeks, who later displayed such a keen sense of history, should have neglected to record their earlier struggles, while Egyptians, who have only recently shown much interest in their history, should in olden times have drawn up so many records of their rulers.

No area of the ancient world, save perhaps Palestine, has been served by such an army of competent scholars as Crete and Mycenaean Greece. In most colleges and universities, all of what is termed "ancient history" has traditionally been turned over to the Classicists, who specialize in Greece and Rome. So it might be expected that the facts available for the Minoan and Mycenaean periods would have been studied intensively and arranged and rearranged in patterns to facilitate the teaching process. Despite all this study and effort, however, many of the basic facts of Minoan and Mycenaean chronology still remain in doubt.

The pre-World War II narrative of Minoan (Cretan) history might be said to have reached its maturity in J. D. S. Pendlebury's *Archaeology of Crete* (1939). Because no earlier cultures had been located on the island, Pendlebury and most other authorities assumed that the Cretans had already reached the Neolithic stage of civilization before they came to Crete. Where did they come from? Pendlebury thought Anatolia was a good possibility because of the evidences of an early connection between that area and Crete. Other authorities thought North Africa was a more probable homeland. All sorts of dates, some as early as 8000 B.C., were suggested for the onset of Neolithic culture in Crete. Pendlebury was uncertain of the date, but noted that measurements of the accumulations of dirt on the floors of Cretan buildings provided a 4100 B.C. origin. With the aid of datable Egyptian artifacts that had been discovered, he ended the Neolithic period in 3000 B.C.

Had the attractive culture on Crete been imported, or developed locally? While Pendlebury traced in detail Crete's connections with Egypt, Mesopotamia, and other places, he seemed convinced that the Minoan culture had evolved on the island through various stages: Early Minoan I-III (3000–2200 B.C.), Middle Minoan I-III (2200–1580 B.C.), and Late Minoan I-III (1580–1250 B.C.). These dates represent a simplified version of a pottery dating system, as old as Sir Arthur Evans's, that often contained subdivisions within the periods.

Pendlebury had to develop a political history out of a few Greek stories and the evidence of three major (and one minor) "destruction levels" that had been unearthed on the island. The Greeks later remembered Minos as a just ruler of Crete, who developed its civilization and codified its laws; but the famous Theseus story represented Minos as a tyrant who demanded a yearly tribute of seven youths and seven maidens to be devoured by the Minotaur in the Labyrinth. In other words, in the Greek memory, Minos had a sort of schizophrenic personality. As for the destruction levels, the major ones were usually dated 1750 B.C., 1580 B.C., and 1400 B.C.

As Pendlebury reconstructed history, Crete had a lengthy and peaceful development until 1750 B.C. when the first earthquake hit. This was a momentary setback, and the culture bloomed even more gloriously until a second earthquake caused widespread destruction in 1580 B.C. Again Crete recovered and went on in the Late Minoan period to establish a thalassocracy, a sea-kingdom that dominated the Aegean, levied tribute on the Greek states, and shut them out from the rich trade with Egypt. There was a minor earthquake during Late Minoan I to which Pendlebury did not attach much importance. The end came suddenly in 1400 B.C. when the Greeks invaded the island with the intention of destroying their rival completely. The evidence for this was the widespread fires at this level. As Pendlebury saw it, the fires were the key to the mystery. In those days before gas lines and electric wires, earthquakes did not cause fires, and the destruction level of 1400 B.C. was a holocaust.

After World War II there was a tendency to downgrade Crete. Some writers moved the Early Minoan period forward to 2600 B.C., and one authority suggested abandoning part of it altogether. Pendlebury had assumed that a single people, who did not change much during the Bronze Age, lived on the island; later writers fancied that a regular goulash of peoples from Anatolia, the Cyclades, and even Syria had settled there. There was nothing suggesting a cultural uniformity during the whole Early Minoan period.

The sensational finds in Anatolia in the 1950s and 1960s accelerated this process of downgrading. Some authorities were convinced that Cretan originality had been overplayed, and others believed the palace of Knossos was a mere copy of an earlier palace at Beycesultan. Meanwhile the translation of Linear B tablets found at Knossos proved that the Greeks were in charge there well before the destruction in 1400 B.C. And, finally, the work of Spyridon Marinatos on the island of Thera in 1967 provided a natural explanation for the great destruction level. A tremendous volcanic explosion on that island, about seventy-five miles north of Crete, had split Thera into three parts, created huge tidal waves, and had sent out mountains of ash. Had Crete been the basis of the Atlantis story?

If one turns to a standard text in Greek history, such as Russell Meiggs' 1975 revision of the J. B. Bury work, hoping to find a story such as Pendlebury and others of his time created, one is likely to come away somewhat disappointed. Meiggs rejected the volcanic destruction theory on the ground that the pottery date for it, 1500 B.C., was too early, and he seriously questioned the existence of a Minoan Empire. Otherwise the account is all too vague, and it is made the more so when the stimulating views of Leonard R. Palmer (*Mycenaeans and Minoans,* 1965) are brought into it. Palmer argued that the Greeks took over Crete in 1400 B.C. and held Knossos until its destruction by the Dorians in the twelfth century.

In view of all this vagueness and confusion, R. F. Willett's *Civilization of Ancient Crete* (1977) was welcome, for he provided a much-needed continuity to the story. The Neolithic origins of the Cretan culture were again assumed in this study and for the same reason as before—no Palaeolithic remains have been found on Crete. Eight C-14 dates, ranging between 6100–3000 B.C., were used in this study to date the Cretan Neolithic, so the reader had something more than floor dirt to stand on. During that lengthy period the Cretan farmers lived mostly on isolated farmsteads. Towards the end of the period, probably as the result of an invasion, village life and finally the Bronze Age came into being. In this study the Early Minoan period was upgraded again. Using the Mesara tombs excavated in 1954–1959 and the Bronze Age settlement at Myrtos which came to light during 1967–1968 as evidence, Willetts concluded that Crete had a thousand years of peace and cultural development.

By the time of this writing, four palaces were known to have existed during the Middle Minoan period, the fourth discovered by Nicholas Platon at Zakros in 1962. These were assumed to be the administrative and religious centers of a well-run state, and Willetts defended the originality of these Cretan structures against all who would trace their inspiration to foreign sources. The cultural influence of Crete was widespread, but Willetts denied that the Minoans had created an empire. Greek invaders destroyed many structures on the island about 1450 B.C. and ruled from Knossos until 1375 B.C. This would account for the schizophrenic personality of Minos in the Greek memory. Before 1450 B.C. he was a wise and just lawgiver and was a tyrant only during the Greek occupation period. Who ousted the Greeks and destroyed Knossos about 1375 B.C. was unknown. While Willetts also tended to be somewhat vague regarding his personal views toward the end of the account, the foregoing is probably a fair statement of Cretan history as he saw it.

It is inaccurate to say that Crete has no history—it is a story still in the process of development. Will a flood of light fall upon the Minoan landscape when the scripts are finally deciphered? Perhaps—and perhaps not. The decipherment of

Linear B has done little to clear up the history of the glorious Mycenaean Age.

When I first encountered Greek history almost a half century ago and began to impart the story to my students after World War II, the outlines of the Mycenaean Age seemed to be fairly definite, as was the earlier history of Greece. Greek history began when the pre-Greek "Pelasgian," or "Aegean," people, who had already reached the Neolithic stage of culture, left their homeland in North Africa or Anatolia and spread into Crete, the Aegean islands, and Greece itself. They were Mediterraneans in ethnic background and spoke a non-Indo-European language which survived in place names with "ss" and "nth" in them. These people created the Minoan culture and the Helladic culture of mainland Greece.

The Early Helladic period (ca. 2500–2000 B.C.) showed a continuous, if not very distinguished, cultural development, then gave way to the Middle Helladic period (ca. 2000–1600 B.C.), which was much more exciting. Early in this period a distinctive grey pottery called "Minyan Ware" appeared and heralded the arrival of the first wave of the Indo-European Greeks. When a people on a lower cultural level enter the environment of a higher culture, they adopt the foreign words necessary to describe their new environment. As the Ionian Greek dialect contained a huge percentage of foreign words, the Ionians were assumed to have been the first wave of Greeks to enter what became their new homeland. For an indefinite period the Ionians and Pelasgians lived together in harmony and profited culturally from their contacts with the more advanced Minoans.

Somewhat later, perhaps around 1700 B.C., the Arcadians and the Aeolians, who together formed the "Achaean" people Homer immortalized, entered Greece. They were made of sterner stuff than the Ionians and drove their predecessors into the less desirable sections of the country while establishing themselves at Tiryns, Mycenae, and other places. They were at times sea raiders, and the shaft graves, rich in gold, were presumably the repositories of the loot acquired by their piratical activities.

At some time during the Middle Helladic period, perhaps in self-defense, the Minoans colonized some Aegean islands and established their sovereignty over Greece. The Achaeans found themselves shut out by the Minoans from the Egyptian trade and from that of the Black Sea by the Trojans. This intolerable situation was ended during the Late Helladic (1600–1100 B.C.) or Mycenaean period when the well-greaved Achaeans destroyed Crete in 1400 B.C. and went on to sack Troy in 1184–1183 B.C. This last date, long an anchor in the period, had been derived from Eratosthenes of Cyrene, who lived in the third century B.C. The rulers of Sparta believed they were descended from the three sons of Hercules, and their king lists extended back to the time they "returned" to Greece. Counting up the generations, Eratosthenes calculated they had returned (by our calendar) in 1104 or 1103 B.C., and it was known that the Trojan War took place two generations before the "return." So eighty years were added to the date of the return, and the fall of Troy was placed in history.

These destructions were only two among similar episodes during the Mycenaean Age. In time, the Achaeans were exhausted by their wars and colonization efforts and fell quickly before the Dorians, the last wave of Greeks to enter the country. The Dorian invasion about 1100 B.C. brought on the "Dark Age," which lasted until about 800 B.C.

This was a good story, full of sound and fury, one which commanded and held the attention of the students. But this account, like that of Crete, has been subjected to considerable modification since World War II, and the one told today, probably more accurate, is somewhat less dramatic.

Greek history did not begin with the Neolithic period. A C-14 sample from Epirus has a date of 40,000 B.C., and other Palaeolithic sites have been located both in Greece and Macedonia. Just when the Neolithic period should begin in Greece proper is fairly definite—in Macedonia it began as early as 6200 B.C., and the settlements in Greece date to the early sixth millennium B.C.

Then came the Bronze Age. Some writers begin the Early Helladic period as far back as 3000 or 2800 B.C., but it is agreed that bronze did not come into general use until 2500 B.C., the traditional opening of this period. There is little change in the scholars' estimate of it. The Early Helladic period, ending in 2000 or 1900 B.C., was simply undistinguished.

The coming of the Greeks into the country named for them is less definite in point of time than scholars once thought. The Minyan Ware that used to be associated with the Ionians has been found in an evolving form at Lerna and other places dating to the Early Helladic period and appears to have been a local development. The "wave theory" has been undermined by scholars who explain the dialectical differences among the Ionians, Aeolians, and Arcadians on purely linguistic grounds.

At least one authority, Moses I. Finley, in his *Early Greece* (1970), was much impressed by the widespread destruction about 2200–2100 B.C. at Tiryns, Lerna, Corinth, and other sites in Greece, not to mention at places in the Cyclades, Troy II, and Beycesultan in southwestern Asia Minor. Finley suggested that this destruction might have been caused by Indo-European invaders, some of whom brought with them a language that eventually evolved into Greek. Friedrich Cornelius believed that some of these Indo-Europeans brought their loot to Alaca Hüyük in Asia Minor.

Despite disputes regarding the date of arrival, it is generally assumed that the Greeks mixed with a pre-Greek population already established in the country and that they were present during the Middle Helladic period (1900–1600 B.C.). Whether they were ever conquered by the Minoans is still uncertain, but the weight of scholarly opinion is heavily against it.

The Late Helladic period (1600–1100), also called the Mycenaean Age, has presented and still presents vexing problems. As early as 1942 Arne Furumark constructed a chronology for this period based on pottery styles, an endeavor which also occupied A. D. Lacy in 1967. They secured approximate dates from Mycenaean pottery discovered in datable Egyptian contexts and Egyptian artifacts of known date found in Mycenaean contexts. On this basis, the period is subdivided into Late Helladic I (1600–1500 B.C.), II (1500–1400 B.C.), IIIA (1400–1300 B.C.), IIIB (1300–1200 B.C.), and IIIC (1200–1100 B.C.). This system of dating has been applied to the destruction of Knossos, and the date derived is circa 1375 B.C. This is an important date in Mycenaean history. Presumably the Greeks occupied the palace before that time —when and how are both unclear.

Dating the sack of Troy by this system has also given rise to extended discussions. The great fortresss of Troy VI, which fitted admirably the description in Homer, used IIIA pottery at the time of its destruction presumably by an earthquake, so the end of this city could have been no later than 1300 B.C., well before the traditional date for the fall. The rebuilt city called Troy VIIA used IIIB pottery and Troy VIIB, IIIC; the former is thought to have existed between 1300–1200 B.C. and the latter, 1200–1100 B.C.

This shift from Helladic IIIB to IIIC is now regarded as of enormous importance in the history of early Greece. Around the year 1200 B.C., Greece was invaded from the north, a dozen palaces and forts were demolished, and, as one writer put it, Greece was "decapitated," deprived of leadership. After this catastrophe some of the Greek cities were abandoned while others continued with a reduced population. Some of the Achaeans fled to Cyprus, others possibly joined the Sea Peoples during the attacks on Egypt. So complete was the destruction culturally that the art of writing was lost, at least some authorities believe it was.

The identity of the people who leveled Greece, according to the traditional account, was well established. They were the late-coming Dorians. Finley points out that the Dorian dialect cannot be explained linguistically as an evolution of Mycenaean Greek, so it must be assumed that Dorians were invaders, but their arrival seems to have come later, probably in the eleventh century B.C. This would rule them out as the force behind the widespread destruction of 1200 B.C. The Dark Age had already settled in before their arrival.

Troy today stands mute and somewhat forlorn. Carl W. Blegen, the outstanding authority on all matters Trojan, placed the destruction of Troy VIIA about 1240 B.C. or perhaps a little earlier. This would leave time for the Greeks to sack it before they, themselves, were sacked and uprooted. But Troy VIIA is an impoverished site, quite unlike the thriving city described by Homer. In view of all this, some writers are ready to go back to pre-Schliemann times and dismiss the *Iliad* as myth.

Our account of the rediscovery of the ancient Near East must end in an all-too-familiar cloud of uncertainty. Much, both important and exciting, has been accomplished during almost two centuries of recovery effort; and more of both undoubtedly lies in prospect. For all who can view this effort in perspective, who have watched the heroic gropings in the dark and the Faustian strivings toward light, there can be only one conclusion—what a splendid intellectual adventure it all has been!

Appendix: Maps

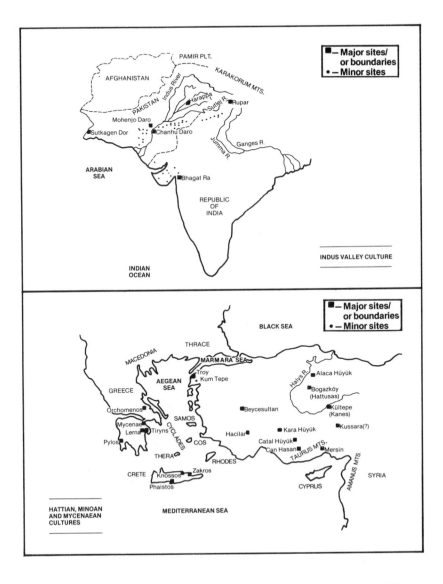

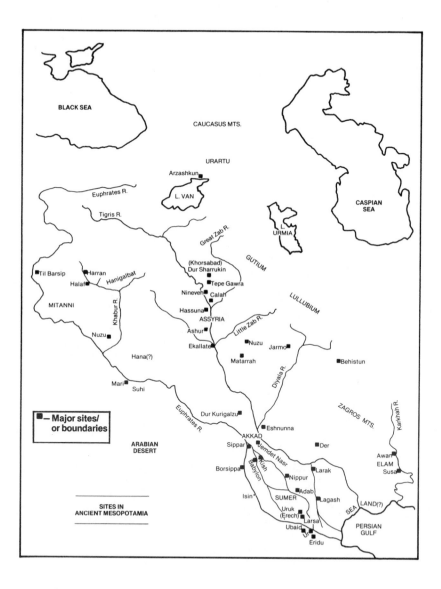

BLACK SEA

CAUCASUS MTS.

URARTU

Arzashkun

Euphrates R.

L. VAN

CASPIAN
SEA

Tigris R.

Great Zab R.

L.
URMIA

GUTIUM

(Khorsabad)
Dur Sharrukin

Til Barsip

Harran

Hanigalbat

Tepe Gawra

LULLUBIUM

Halaf

Nineveh

Calah

MITANNI

Khabur R.

Hassuna

ASSYRIA

Nuzu

Ashur

Little Zab R.

Ekallate

Nuzu

Jarmo

Hana(?)

Matarrah

Diyala R.

Behistun

Mari

Suhi

ZAGROS MTS.

Karkhah R.

Euphrates R.

Dur Kurigalzu

■— Major sites/
or boundaries

Eshnunna

ARABIAN
DESERT

AKKAD

Der

Sippar

Jemdet Nasr

Awan
ELAM

Borsippa

Kish

Susa

Babylon

Larak

Nippur

Isin

Adab

SUMER

Lagash

SITES IN
ANCIENT MESOPOTAMIA

Uruk
(Erech)

SEA LAND(?)

Larsa

Ubaid

PERSIAN
GULF

Eridu

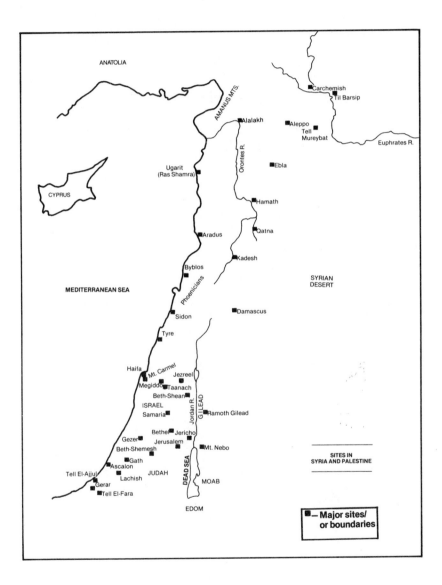

ANATOLIA

Carchemish
Til Barsip

AMANUS MTS.

Alalakh

Aleppo
Tell
Mureybat

Euphrates R.

Orontes R.

Ugarit
(Ras Shamra)

Ebla

CYPRUS

Hamath

MEDITERRANEAN SEA

Aradus

Qatna

Byblos

Kadesh

Phoenicians

SYRIAN
DESERT

Sidon

Damascus

Tyre

Haifa

Mt. Carmel

Jezreel

Megiddo

Taanach

Beth-Shean

ISRAEL

Samaria

Jordan R.

GILEAD

Ramoth Gilead

Bethel

Jericho

Gezer

Jerusalem

Beth-Shemesh

Mt. Nebo

Gath

Ascalon

Tell El-Ajjul

JUDAH

DEAD SEA

Lachish

MOAB

Gerar

Tell El-Fara

EDOM

SITES IN
SYRIA AND PALESTINE

■ — Major sites/
or boundaries

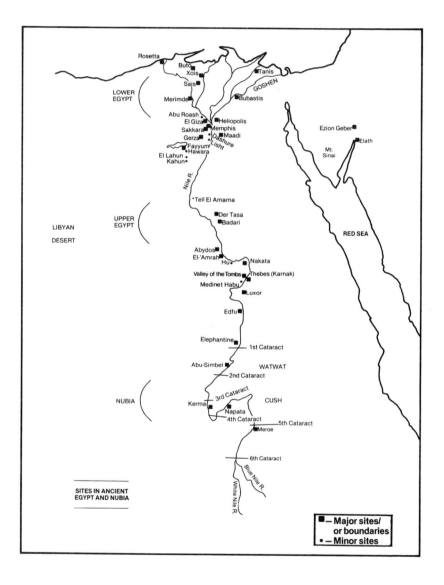

SITES IN ANCIENT
EGYPT AND NUBIA

140

Annotated
Bibliography:

Books for Ancient Near Eastern History Buffs

Many of the older American libraries reflect the nineteenth
century interest in the ancient Near East and display such
works as James Henry Breasted, *A History of Egypt* (New
York: Charles Scribner's Sons, 1905), Leonard W. King, *A
History of Sumer and Akkad* (London: Chatto and Windus,
1910), Gaston C. C. Maspero, *The Struggle of the Nations*
(New York: D. Appleton and Co., 1897), and Robert W.
Rogers, *A History of Babylonia and Assyria* (New York:
Easton and Mains, 1900). Often written in a leisurely style,
such works provide an introduction to the historiography of
the area as well as interesting interpretations and stray facts.

General histories of the ancient Near East are few in number. The best-known is Harry R. R. Hall's *The Ancient History of the Near East from the Earliest Times to the Battle of
Salamis* (London: Methuen & Co., 1911), last revision, 1950.
Written well before the discoveries in Syria especially forced
major revisions of Near Eastern history, it is of limited value
today. William F. Albright's survey called *From the Stone
Age to Christianity* (Baltimore: Johns Hopkins Press, 1957)

is less political than cultural and religious. More recently the earlier half of the history was covered by Jean Bottero et al. in *The Near East: The Early Civilizations* (New York: Delacorte Press, 1965), a work that students find valuable and fairly current.

Those searching for a solid political history of Egypt will want to read Sir Alan Gardiner, *Egypt of the Pharaohs* (Oxford: Clarendon Press, 1961). Cyril Aldred's *The Egyptians* (New York: Frederick A. Praeger, 1961) is much less concerned with dates and chronology. *The Splendour That Was Egypt* (New York: Philosophical Library, 1949) by Margaret A. Murray employs the Petrie chronology and displays an interest in social history. George Steindorff and Keith C. Seele, *When Egypt Ruled the East* (Chicago: University of Chicago Press, 1947) presents a lively account especially of the Empire period. One of the most popular and interpretative studies ever written about ancient Egypt is John Albert Wilson's *The Burden of Egypt* (Chicago: University of Chicago Press, 1951).

The Tigris-Euphrates Valley area has attracted fewer writers than the Nile. Svend A. Pallis, *The Antiquity of Iraq* (Copenhagen: Ejnar Muntesgaard, Ltd., 1956) covers its history from earliest times down through Chaldaean Babylonia. It employs the Smith chronology.

Some of the works on Sumer from the 1920s have been reissued or revised in recent times, such as Cyril J. Gadd, *History and Monuments of Ur* (New York: Benjamin Blom, 1972) and C. Leonard Woolley, *Excavations at Ur* (New York: Barnes and Noble, 1963). Samuel Noah Kramer, *The Sumerians: Their History, Culture, and Character* (Chicago: University of Chicago Press, 1964) is a political and cultural history by an outstanding authority in the field.

Few recent works on Babylonia and Assyria are available, though there are plenty of old ones. H. W. F. Saggs, *The Greatness That Was Babylon* (New York: Praeger, 1969) provides a short history of Babylon from earliest times to the

Persian conquest, but spends more space on Babylonian culture. Albert Ten Eyck Olmstead's *History of Assyria* (New York: Charles Scribner's Sons, 1923) is still the outstanding political treatment as well as the strongest defense of the Assyrians in history. Interesting sidelights on Assyrian government in the second millennium are found in Jorgen Laessoe, *Peoples of Ancient Assyria* (New York: Barnes and Noble, 1963). Georges Contenau, *Everyday Life in Babylon and Assyria* (New York: St. Martin's Press, 1954) is a somewhat disappointing treatment of the social history of the two states.

Recent works on the Hittites are fairly abundant. A deservedly popular earlier work in this area is Oliver R. Gurney, *The Hittites* (Baltimore: Penguin Books, 1964). One of the more easily read and up-to-date works, particularly strong for the archaeological period, is Johannes Lehmann, *The Hittites: People of a Thousand Gods* (New York: Viking Press, 1977).

For obvious reasons, Palestine has inspired a large number of studies, and the student has a wide choice of offerings. Emmanuel Anati, *Palestine Before the Hebrews* (New York: Alfred A. Knopf, 1963) is an interesting archaeological account. Harold H. Rowley's, *From Joseph to Joshua* (Oxford: University Press, 1950) is a treasure house of theories relating to the early history of the Hebrews; the recently revised *A History of Israel* (Philadelphia: Westminister Press, 1972) by John Bright covers a longer period. Those who seek naturalistic explanations for biblical miracles can find them in Werner Keller, *The Bible as History* (New York: W. Morrow, 1956).

This writer does not know of a history of Syria devoted entirely to the ancient period. Horst Klengel, *The Art of Ancient Syria* (New York: A. S. Barnes and Co., 1972) describes some of the important historical sites in that country, but it is chiefly pictorial. Sir Charles L. Woolley's *A Forgotten Kingdom* (London: M. Parrish, 1959) describes Alalakh and its predecessors. Gerhard Herm, *The Phoenicians*

(London: Victor Gollancz, 1975) is an effective treatment of a people neighboring Syria.

There is little to say about the mute Indus Valley civilization. The classical work on the subject is Sir Robert E. M. Wheeler's *Civilizations of the Indus Valley and Beyond* (New York: McGraw-Hill, 1966). A broader study is *The Roots of Ancient India* (New York: Macmillan, 1971) by Walter Ashlin Fairservis, Jr.

Many outstanding monographic studies are available, particularly for Egypt. One of the more recent books about King Tut is Cyril Aldred, *Tutankhamun's Egypt* (London: British Broadcasting Corp., 1972), a popular work by a recognized scholar. Edward Fay Campbell, Jr. in *The Chronology of the Amarna Letters* (Baltimore: Johns Hopkins Press, 1964) clarifies many complex details of Egyptian diplomacy during the Amarna era. Kenneth A. Kitchen, *The Third Intermediate Period in Egypt, 1100–650* B.C. (Warminster: Aris & Phillips, 1973) faces up to difficult chronological problems, not without some success. Donald B. Redford in his *History and Chronology of the Eighteenth Dynasty of Egypt* (Toronto: University Press, 1967) takes sharp issue with some of Wilson's interpretations. In *The Hyksos: A New Investigation* (New Haven: Yale University Press, 1966), John Van Seters considers this problem within a broad scholarly context. Those interested in Egyptian literature should consult Miriam Lichtheim, *Ancient Egyptian Literature: The Old and Middle Kingdoms* (Berkeley: University of California Press, 1973), while devotees of art will probably find Cyril Aldred, *The Development of Ancient Egyptian Art from 3200 to 1315* (London: A. Tiranti, 1962) to be outstanding.

Monographs involving the Tigris-Euphrates area are less abundant. Ephraim A. Speiser's *Mesopotamian Origins, the Basic Population of the Near East* (Philadelphia: University of Pennsylvania Press, 1930) is still a classic work, though the author later modified some of his conclusions. No work, either, has replaced George C. Cameron's *The History of*

Early Iran (Chicago: University of Chicago Press, 1936), which provides a detailed history of the Elamites. Alfred Halder's *Who Were the Amorites?* (Leiden: E. J. Brill, 1971) should be read by all those interested in early Babylonian history. Thomas B. Jones, *The Sumerian Problem* (New York: John Wiley and Sons, 1969) discusses in detail the factors in the Sumerian controversy.

Certain monographs dealing with miscellaneous subjects might also be mentioned. I. M. Diakonoff, ed., *Ancient Mesopotamia: Socio-Economic History* (Moscow: Nauka Publishing House, 1969) contains articles by Marxist historians who attempt to shape early history into their accepted pattern. Though a dull work, one is pleased to find a slight tendency to overcome the presuppositions forced on them by their ideology. Brian M. Fagan, *The Rape of the Nile, Tomb Robbers, Tourists and Archaeologists in Egypt* (New York: Charles Scribner's Sons, 1975) takes note of the practices deplored in the present work. Graduate students usually enthusiastic about Henri Frankfort, *The Intellectual Adventure of Ancient Man* (Chicago: University of Chicago Press, 1946). James E. Harris and Kent R. Weeks, *X-Raying the Pharaohs* (New York: Charles Scribner's Sons, 1975) describe this interesting attempt by modern science to pry into the past. Ilse Seibert, *Women in the Ancient Near East* (New York: Abner Schram, 1974) is a pictorial study which should interest feminists. Those attracted by the Neolithic age will be interested in the essays in Stuart Struever, ed., *Prehistoric Agriculture* (Garden City: Natural History Press, 1971).

It is often refreshing to read some of the original sources of ancient Near Eastern history. A splendid collection of documents from many areas is found in James B. Pritchard, *Ancient Near Eastern Texts Relating to the Old Testament* (Princeton: Princeton University Press, 1955) as well as in his subsequent publications. The title is somewhat misleading; most of the documents are only remotely related to the Bible. The collection of Sumerian documents in Samuel Noah

Kramer, *From the Tablets of Sumer* (Indian Hills: Falcon's Wing Press, 1956) proves the many contributions to civilization of this early people. Biblical scholars should be interested in D. J. Wiseman, *Chronicles of the Chaldaean Kings, 626–556* (London: Trustees of the British Museum, 1956) which tells much of what we know about Nabu-kudurri-usur and others of his time. A. Leo Oppenheim in *Letters from Mesopotamia* (Chicago: University of Chicago Press, 1967) quotes from communications from the Agade period down through the end of the Assyrian Empire.

Those who desire to keep up with developments in this area must go to the scholarly journals, which, alas, often contain articles quite incomprehensible to those with a limited command of languages. Prominent among these publications are the *Bulletin of the American Schools of Oriental Research,* the *Journal of Egyptian Archaeology,* and the *Journal of Cuneiform Studies.* I have found the *Journal of Near Eastern Studies,* published by the Oriental Institute of the University of Chicago, to be particularly helpful.

Index

Aahmes. *See* Ahmose
Abadiyeh, 37
Abraham, 4, 98–99
Abu Habba. *See* Sippara
Abu Roash, 14
Abu Shahrain. *See* Eridu
Abusir, 14
Abydos list, 19–20, 39, 73
Achaeans, 131–32, 134
Adab, 42
Adad-nirari III, 24
Aemilianus, Scipio, 1–2
Aeolians, 131–33
Africa, 11, 15
Africanus, Sextus Julius, 6
Agade, 30, 82–83
Agamemnon, 32
Age of Reason, 10
Agum II, 106
Agumkagrime Chronicle, 28, 106
Ahab, 109, 111
Ahaz, 111
Ahmose (Aahmes) I, 93–94
Akerblad, Johan D., 54–55
Akhenaten. *See* Amenhotep IV
Akkad, 2, 22, 81, 120
Akkadian language, 63, 65
Alaca Hüyük, 126, 133
Alalakh, 39, 46, 103, 107
Albright, William F., 92, 99,
    102, 104–7, 110, 112, 124
Aldred, Cyril, 95–96
Alexandria, 12
Alkim, U Bahadir, 126
Amarna tablets, 21, 48, 68, 101
Amaziah, 111
Ambrose, Saint, 9
Amélineau, M. E., 20–21, 39
Amenemhat (Ammenemes) III,
    45, 93
Amenemhat IV, 45

Amenhotep (Amenophis) I,
    20, 78–79, 93, 97
Amenhotep II, 20
Amenhotep III, 20, 40
Amenhotep (Akhenaten) IV,
    40, 100
Ammi-zaduga, 86, 103
Amorities, 82, 87
Amraphel, 98–99
Amratian culture, 119–20
Amur-pi-el, 99
Anati, Emmanuel, 124
Anatolia, 125–26, 129, 131
Anquetil-Dupperon, Abraham
    H., 60
Apiru. *See* Habiru
Arabs, 4, 8, 12, 14–15
Arcadians, 131, 133
Archaeology, modern, 38–39,
    116–19
Arioch, 98–99
Arlotto, Anthony, 65
Armageddon. *See* Megiddo
Arpad, 47
Arzawa, 48, 68
Asa, 111
Ascalon, 45
Asher, 101–2
Ashur (Kalaat-Sherghat), 41
Ashurbanipal, 25, 27–28, 64,
    84, 109
Ashur-dan III, 109
Ashur-etil-ilani, 24
Ashur-nadin-ahhe I, 104
Ashur-rabi I, 104
Assyria, 1, 4, 7, 21–23, 28, 41,
    46, 103, 109, 112, 125
Assyrian cuneiform, 63, 65
Assyrian king lists, 87, 104–8
Atlantis, 129
Avesta, 59–60
Azariah, 27, 111

Babel, 28
Babylon I dynasty, 42, 46, 82–86,
    99, 103–5, 109–10
Babylonians, 2, 6, 21–23,

147